Memories *of a* Barefoot Boy

Dale R. Wright, Sr.

Memories of a Barefoot Boy
Dale R. Wright, Sr.

Contact the author: ricoshay10@gmail.com

Published and Edited by:

Mary Ethel

Mary Ethel Eckard
Frisco, Texas

Library of Congress Control Number: 2025915596
ISBN (Print): 978-1-966561-18-7
ISBN (E-book): 978-1-966561-19-4

Dedication

To my grandchildren
Ray Patrick McMillen, Heather Winters,
J.C. McMillen, and Travis Neyland Wright

And to my great grandchildren
Brenly, Avery, Rowan, Olivia, James, Wright,
Tripp, Talon, and Teagan

And to all those who will come into our family
years and generations after I have
gone to be with the Lord.

May God bless you and keep you, and
may you always seek His face.
He is the One who is faithful through it all!

CONTENTS

PREFACE

In the following stories, I have attempted to write some of the memories of my childhood. Because some of my memories are so vague, most of these stories are brief. For this I apologize.

Until I was about 12 years old, my world was very small. It consisted of the house we lived in and an area about 2 to 3 miles around it. It was about a mile to the nearest home and family from our house.

The little town of Roganville was about a mile away. This town was started by John Henry Kirby who built a sawmill there. When he built a sawmill, he usually built houses and a general store. The mill and houses were gone when I was old enough to remember. It left a big open grassy area and a mill pond. It was called the Mill yard. This mill yard was used by folks who let their cattle run free and was a great dove hunting place during the fall.

When I walked to town, I would sometimes cut across some of the open area just to explore. But if the big white Brama bull that roamed the area with cows was visible, I went way around him. I gave him plenty of room.

There was also a small branch stream that ran through the mill yard. It was always fun to explore around it, even though I had been told by my mom to stay away from the bridge that crossed the branch. There was also a creek bridge to cross going to town. Will talk more about the creek later.

In reading these events, if it sometimes seems to sound like a difficult life because of the environment and lack of modern things, I did not intend to imply that. Yes, we had less than some, but more than others. I never gave thought to why we did not have things that others did. I was happy.

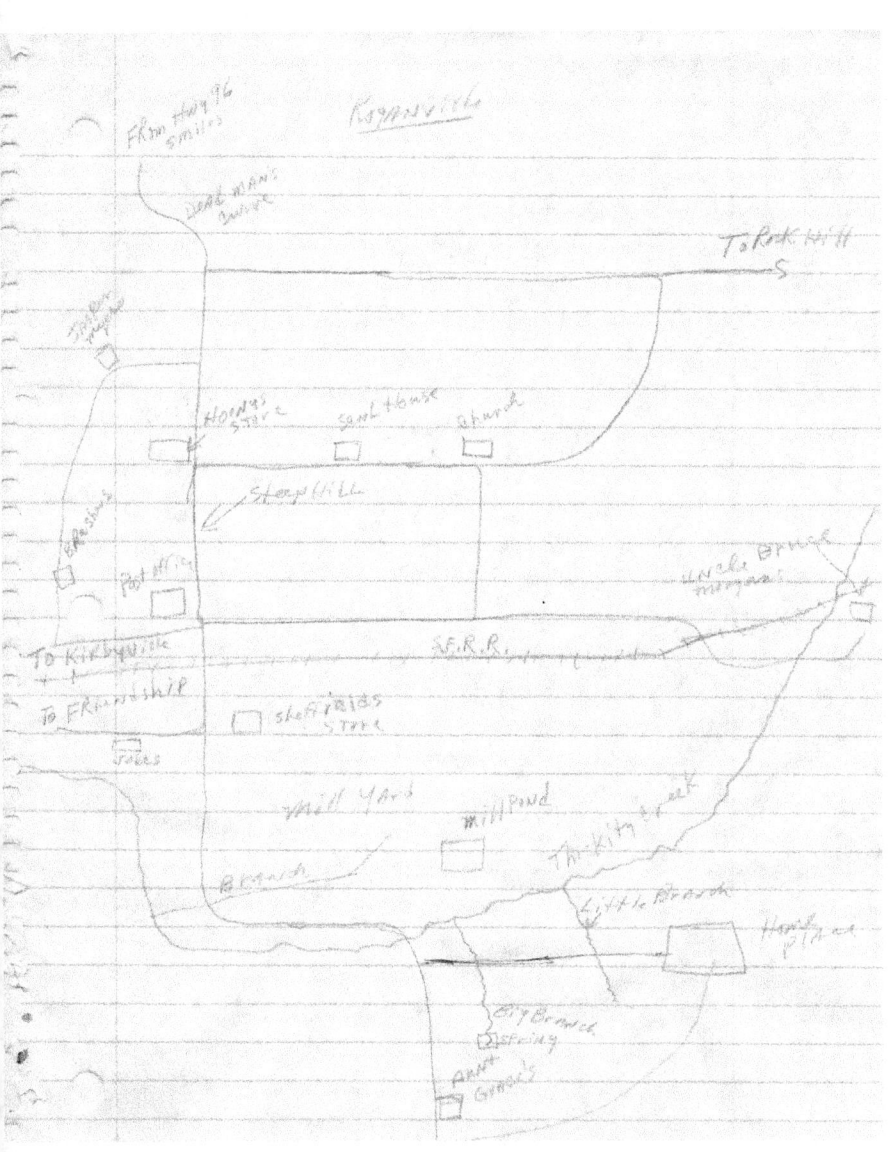

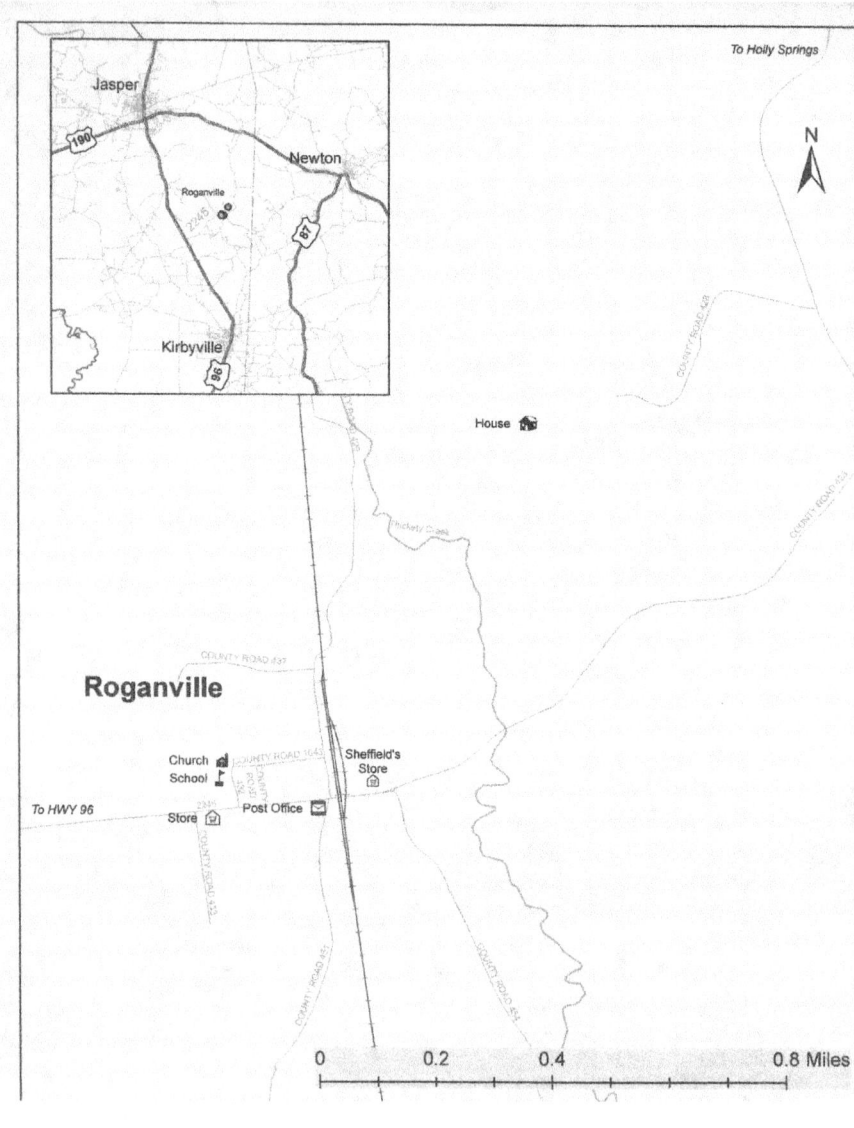

To Holly Springs

N

Jasper

190

Newton

Roganville

87

Kirbyville

86

House

Hickory Creek

COUNTY ROAD 697

Roganville

Church
School

COUNTY ROAD 1043

Sheffield's
Store

To HWY 96

Store

Post Office

| 0 | 0.2 | 0.4 | 0.8 Miles |

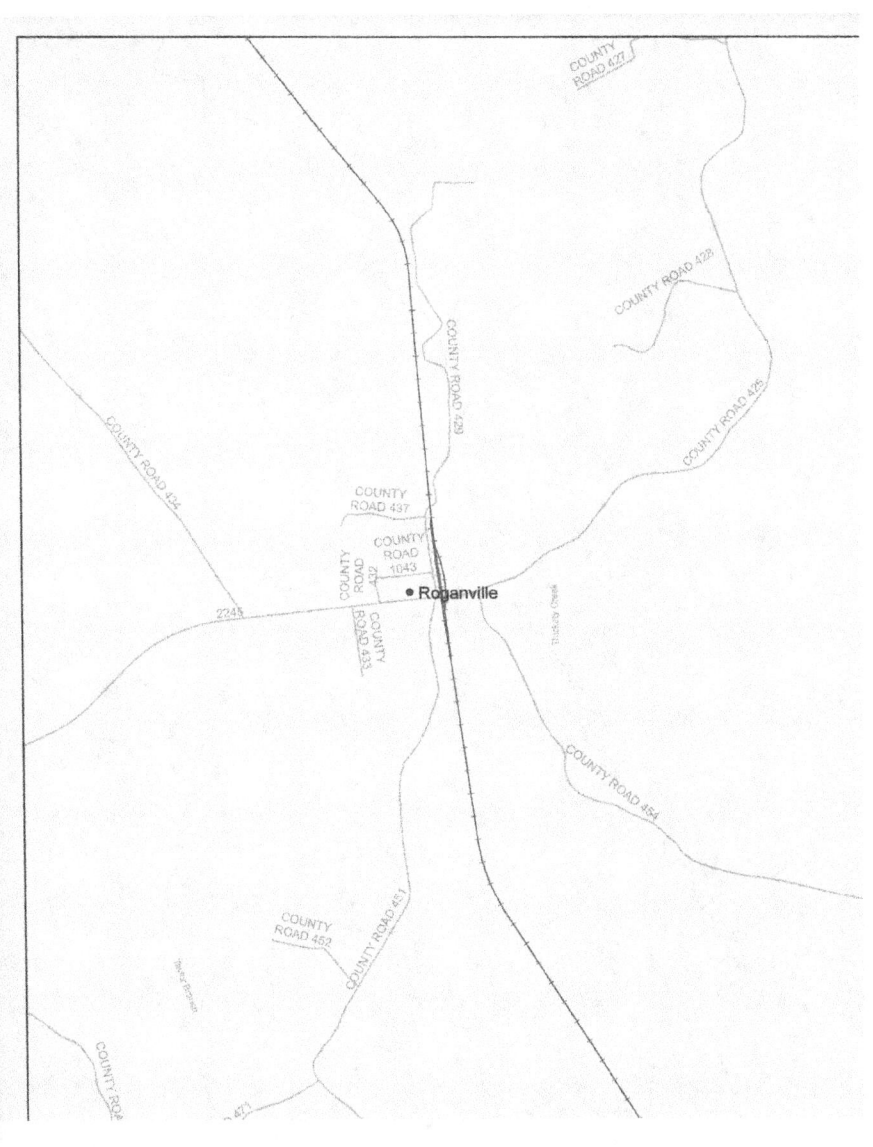

The House

We lived in a house that my grandfather built many years before. It was the type of house with a hall that ran from the front porch to the back porch. There were 3 bedrooms on one side of the hall, and the kitchen and living room on the other side. The hall was not closed in.

The front porch was not used very much, but the back porch had rocking chairs to sit in.

The yard around the house did not have any grass in it. If grass did come up, it had to be removed with a hoe. When leaves and other trash accumulated in the yard, it had to be swept with a brush broom. The brush broom was made from small limbs of dogwood trees. The limbs were tied together at a few places. It worked well.

The water supply for the house was a well adjacent to the house at the back near the kitchen door. There was a door in the kitchen that opened right next to the well. Water was drawn from the well with a bucket on a pully.

On the back porch, there was a shelf with a water bucket. A dipper hung on the wall next to the left end of the shelf. Sometimes it was a gourd dipper, and we also had a metal dipper. Also on the shelf was a pan for washing hands and face. Of course, there was a bar of homemade lye soap in a dish. A towel hung on the post at the right end of the shelf.

In comparison to today, it would be considered primitive living. As a boy, I didn't know any better. I thought life was fun.

I was about 5 years old when we moved into the house so my mom could take care of her dad. This part of my life is fuzzy. I don't remember the details very well.

The house was on piers a few feet high so there was a lot of space under the house. That was one of my play areas. I would make roads for my cars and trucks. My cars were usually old brown snuff bottles. These bottles were square and made good toy cars. My roads I made under the house didn't get torn down, since only me and the dog would go under there. I guess I must have gotten pretty dirty.

As I grew, I continued to roam a little further into the woods around the house. I remember I had to be close enough to hear my mom when she called me, or I was in serious trouble. Trouble sometimes meant being introduced to a switch from a bridal wreath bush that grew right by the front porch. Many times, I thought about how I could cut that thing down without anyone knowing I did it. Never did try that.

One of my favorite places to spend time was a small branch of water that was a few hundred yards from the house. I enjoyed building dams across the little stream to create a little pool and playing with boats made from leaves. Magnolia leaves made excellent boats.

Routine Chores

I did have numerous chores to do. In addition, I needed to be where mother could call me if she needed me to do something. Of course, the chores changed as I grew older.

It was my job to keep wood for Mother's kitchen stove. There was a wood box by the stove. It was not supposed to get empty. That was explained to me often.

If you are familiar with a wood stove, then you know the wood had to be small and a certain length to fit in the firebox. It had to be dry, and it couldn't be pine because pine creates a lot of smoke.

There was usually a stack of stove wood a little way from the front porch. My older brother and my dad would either cut the wood and haul it home or bring uncut pieces to cut and split.

To start the fire each morning, there had to be some kindling to get it going. Kindling was usually rich lighter pine that was cut into splinters. This wood had so much turpentine in it that it would start burning with a match.

As we roamed the woods, when we found a piece of a pine tree that had all rotted away except the center or heart of the tree, it became rich lighter pine. It would not rot. It could be cut in slivers with an axe or hatchet to use for kindling.

There will be more stories about cutting and gathering firewood.

Drawing Water From the Well

Another of my jobs was to listen for my dad's car coming up the road in the evening. As it was nearing, I would draw a fresh bucket of water from the well so Dad could have a fresh drink of water when he got home.

This was especially important during the summer, because the water from the well was quite cold (probably about 72 degrees). After he had drank his fill and washed his hands and face, the water bucket was about empty. So, I had to go back to the well to draw more water. I realize now that I did not help as much as I should have.

When Mother was going to wash, if I was around, she would ask for help to draw water from the well. Much too often she would not ask for help when she should have.

Roads to the House

(Refer to the maps in the front of the book as needed to understand where things are.)

There were two roads to get from Roganville to the house. Both roads connected with the Holly Springs Road.

The longer road went straight after crossing the creek bridge for about a couple of miles before turning off. The shorter one turned left just after crossing the creek bridge. One was at least a mile longer than the other. The longer one turned off the Holly Springs Road just past my aunt and uncle's house. The longer road never became impassable because of weather. The road ran through some thick woods.

One did have to be careful because this road was used only when the shorter one was impassable. It had several old logging roads branching off into the woods. If anyone turned on one of these, it probably would end with no turnaround space. The family and friends knew the roads well, so it was only important if they were telling a stranger how to get to the house.

The shorter road started just after crossing the creek bridge. It sort of followed the creek part of the way to the house. It was only about three fourths of a mile from the creek bridge to the house.

The problem was there was a muddy place that seldom went dry. This place spanned from one side of the road to the other. I do not know how many times my dad stuck a vehicle because he thought it was dry enough to cross. Someone once tried to make a little detour around this mudhole, but the land was soft on both sides and had some large trees.

Right at the edge of this mudhole a large spring-fed branch crossed the road. That was probably the reason this place stayed so wet. We called this stream Big Branch. The branch was about eight to ten feet wide in most places.

Where cars crossed the branch, it had a sandy bottom that was solid enough to drive through, but one had to get through or around the mudhole and then turn to miss a couple of big trees to get to the crossing spot. There was plenty of room, but one had to accelerate to get through the mudhole. It was a problem any way someone tried to drive a car through there.

My dad was determined to try and beat this muddy place that caused him to have to drive a few miles further to get home. If he tried to go through there with my mom in the car, she would fuss and tell him that she was not going to get muddy if he stuck the car.

If the car got stuck in the mudhole, it was almost impossible to get out without getting shoes or feet muddy. Mom would tell him, "If you stick this car, you will carry me to dry ground. I am not getting muddy today." Occasionally, Dad would get a running start and get through the edge of the mudhole and barely miss a tree and then cross the branch without getting stuck. But sometimes he would turn around and go the longer way home.

After passing Big Branch, the elevation began to change to higher and drier ground. The road was leaving the "creek bottom." I remember this area being nice and peaceful. The road was wider with large trees on both sides. This was also where a walking trail joined the road. This trail was from north of the house. It was used by folks living north of us that did not have cars to get to town. More about this trail later.

A little further on the road there was another small branch to drive through, but it was not muddy. It had a hard bottom and was called "Little Branch."

Past Little Branch, the road started up a long slow hill that led to an area just away from the house that had been a field many years before. This area was full of small pine trees. The road passed where the house I was born in had been. My memory of this house is almost nonexistent. I remember playing on a porch with a metal truck. My sister told me I knocked myself out by throwing this toy in the air, and it fell on my head.

The road continued up a hill through the pine saplings. This part of the road was very sandy. Evidently, when this was a field, it was probably a very good soil to grow things.

As the road came out of the saplings approaching the house, there was a large domestic mulberry tree that grew about fifty or so feet from the back porch. We did not park cars under this tree when it had berries on it. The berries would drop on anything under the tree and leave a purple blotch.

When the berries were ripe, I loved to climb the tree and eat the purple berries. I was constantly told not to eat them because they had worms in them. I could not see any worms, and the berries were good. Mom could always tell when I had been eating the berries because my mouth was purple. Another lecture about what I had been told about the mulberries.

Uncle Bruce Morgan

There was a trail through the woods that crossed the branch where I enjoyed spending time playing. The trail led through the woods to my great uncle Bruce Morgan's house. His house was about three fourths of a mile away by the trail. I loved going there because Uncle Bruce raised goats. There were always some of them that liked to be petted. I was older before I was allowed to go there alone.

I can remember walking with my grandfather, Manley Morgan, to his brother's house because my grandfather was losing his sight and needed someone to guide him so he would not get lost.

One time we were on our way to Uncle Bruce's and I was probably walking beside the trail so I could keep Papa on the right path. I must have stepped on the opening to their underground den. All at once it seemed like the air was full of yellow jackets. Each one trying to sting me. I began running and yelling for Papa to stay where he was. I didn't want him to wander off the trail.

After running a little way, I dropped down on my belly and the yellow jackets kept flying, I guess. Any way they stopped stinging me.

I got up and I still remember how much the stings were hurting, but I knew I had to get Papa so he would not wander off. I remember we turned around and headed back to the house. My mom mixed up something and put it on the stings. She said she counted 32 stings. I am not likely to forget that trip to Uncle Bruce's. Later as I walked the same trail, I always went off the trail at that place. I had enough yellow jackets to last me a while.

A Trip Home From Magnolia Springs

My aunt Mae and Uncle Webster Horn lived in Magnolia Springs. It was a community about 15 miles from home.

It was always fun for me when we went and visited. They had a boy near my age. His name was Kenneth. We were about 10 years old.

His family lived mostly on what they raised. They had cows for milk and meat. They raised hogs for meat also. My uncle had fields of corn, peas, and beans. They also had a garden for things like tomatoes, peppers, onions, and other vegetables. So there was always something neat for me to see and do. And my aunt was a good cook. She and Mother would cook a meal while they visited.

I need to get back to the story of the trip back home to Roganville. The road we traveled was a paved road. It crossed highway 96 about halfway to Roganville.

At that time, Dad had a pickup of sorts. It was a 1941 Ford. Someone had removed the body and constructed a wooden body on the car frame. There were no doors on the cab. The bed of the vehicle did not have a tailgate. I rode in the back and naturally, being a boy, I sat on the end of the bed with my feet dangling. I mostly was holding on.

When we came to the highway 96 crossing, Dad stopped and then when he started with a jerk, I just slid off the end of the bed onto the road. I did not even fall but stayed on my feet. I was in the middle of the highway crossing. My first thought was, are cars coming? Luckily there were none coming.

I ran on across the highway waving my arms and yelling, hoping Dad or Mom would see me. They didn't. It was 5 miles to Roganville. All I could think about was the long walk ahead of me.

As luck would have it, a man from Roganville came along going toward town before I had walked very far. He recognized me and offered me a ride. He sure did laugh when I told him what happened. The laugh did not make me feel very good about myself.

We had not gone many miles, and we saw the old wooden vehicle coming toward us. So, the gentleman waved Dad down and when he stopped beside the car we were in, he asked Dad if he had lost something. The answer sounded a lot like I might be in trouble.

Things worked out fine. I was lectured but not punished. I can assure you that when I rode in the back of the truck, I did not sit on the very back. I had learned the value of holding on.

After becoming a parent, I know now Mom and Dad must have been frantic with worry when they saw I was not in the truck.

Fishing trip to
Thickety Creek

Thickety Creek ran within a quarter mile of our house. It was a spring fed stream with lots of perch and redeye bass in it. They were called redeye because they have a red ring around the pupil of their eyeballs. (I have since learned they are called Mountain Bass in areas further north.)

These bass did not get very large. Most were about 1 to 3 pounds, but they were fierce fighters. They tasted excellent when cleaned and fried. My mom was extra good at cooking them.

One morning she told me she was "fish hungry" and suggested I go catch some bass. That was right down my alley. That is much better than cutting stove wood or wood for the wash pot.

There were two ways we caught these bass in the creek. One way was to dig earthworms for bait to catch spot tailed shiners and use them for bass bait. The other was to use a rod and reel. I had a three-foot-long steel rod with a casting reel. That was what I was using that day. My older sister had purchased it for me. I had an artificial bait called a Rainbow Minnow. This bait had 5 sets of treble hooks, so if a bass tried to bite it, he was hooked.

Now this was my dad's favorite bait. I knew that if I hung it up on something, I would have to get it, even if it meant swimming under water to get it loose.

The creek was brushy and there was very little room to cast an artificial bait. This was during warm weather, so I waded up the edges of the creek as quiet as I could and made small casts into deeper spots as I came upon them. I was wading in water up to knee deep in places. As I caught a bass, I would put it on a stringer that I had tied to my belt. The stringer floated along, keeping the fish in the water. I would occasionally have to get out of the creek because it would get too deep to wade.

I had been fishing for a while and had quite a few bass on the stringer. As I waded, it kept hanging up on something and I would reach back and jerk the stringer loose. Finally, I was in a clear part with nothing for the stringer to hang on, but it kept hanging up anyway. I stopped and turned around and started lifting the stringer to see what it was hanging on. When I lifted the stringer, there was a four-foot long water moccasin trying to eat my fish. At times he had been rather close to my legs without me knowing it. Needless to say, it didn't take me long to get out of the creek and head home with my fish.

Below is a picture of the old Rainbow Minnow bait. It's the last one my dad bought. I still have it. It is illegal to use in Texas and maybe elsewhere. Conservationists say it has too many hooks, but you never lose a fish after hooking one.

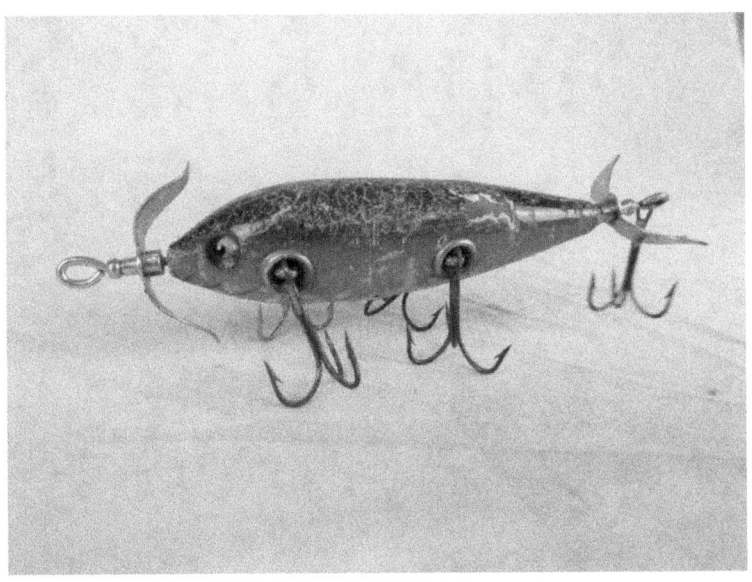

Figure 1 Dad's Rainbow Minnow bait

Getting a Haircut

We had a barber in Roganville. His name was Jasper Myers. As with all adults, I only knew him as Mr. Myers. In that age, a child did not ask what an adult's first name was. A boy could get in serious trouble for addressing an adult by his or her first name, even if you happened to know it.

I never understood why a haircut was necessary in the wintertime. My head was warmer if it had plenty of hair on it. I would have been perfectly happy without ever getting a haircut in winter. My parents felt differently. If the hair was touching the tops of my ears, my dad or mom would mention that it was time to get a haircut.

There were two reasons why I was not thrilled to get a haircut. The barber had no electricity at his house. He cut hair outside under an open shed. Not only was it cold outside in the barber's chair, but he cut hair with a pair of manual clippers that he operated by squeezing them for each cut. As his hand would get tired, he would push up more and seemed to me like the clippers pulled out about as many hairs as they cut.

As the haircut went on, he would cut some with his shears. That was okay. I liked to hear the clicking sound of the shears as he cut hair near my ears. When the clippers would pull the hair, I sometimes could not sit still. The barber would ask me to hold still, and Dad would insist that I be still, even when the hairs were pulled out by the clippers. I would say out loud that it hurt. I was told to hush, because Dad said it was not hurting, that it was just my imagination

What Dad did not say was that he always asked the barber to use only shears on his hair. I was never brave enough to mention this.

When the haircut was finally about over, the barber would sometimes shave the back of my neck. I enjoyed that, it felt good. His straight razor was always sharp and did not pull. Sometimes Dad would say, "Don't worry about shaving his neck, just use the real fine clipper blade." I almost groaned out loud, because the barber would hurry with the fine clippers and they would pull the fine hairs on the back of my neck something fierce.

When he was finished, I jumped out of that barber's chair as fast as I could. But I had better remember to tell the barber thank you or I was in more trouble.

If it was in the summer, as we went home, I would try to get Dad to stop somewhere along Thickety Creek and let me strip and shake the hair out of my shirt. Then get in the creek to rinse the loose hair off. When we got home my mom would always brag about how good my haircut looked.

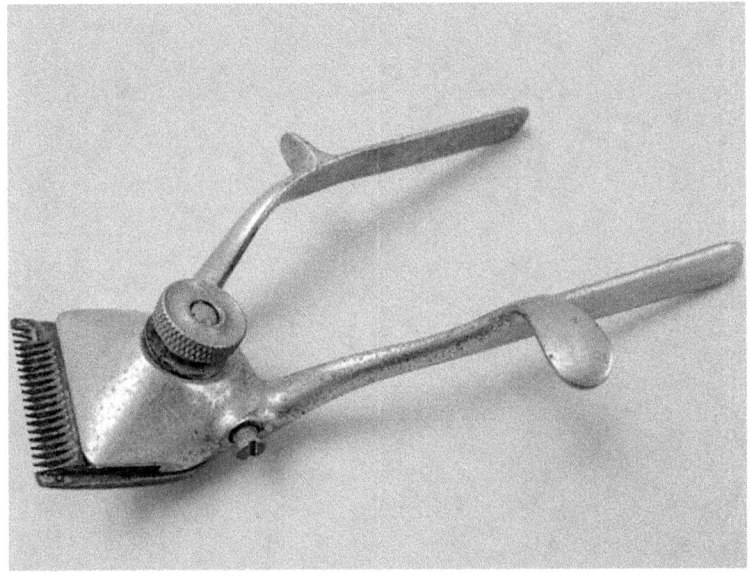

Figure 2 Vintage Hair Clippers

Once When I Did Not Do
What Was Expected Of Me

When I was about 10 or 11, most things I did were outlined by the force in my life, my mother. She would give me a lot of freedom to do as I wanted as long as I stayed in the limits she set around my actions. Not very often did I have to ask if I could do something. I knew very well what my boundaries were. Did I always stay within the boundaries of what I knew was expected of me? Not exactly. I was a young boy with all kinds of ideas of things I wanted to do, and most times, I had an idea of how I wanted to do them. Boy, that did cause me some grief at times.

Here is the context for this story. It was a Sunday morning. I had gotten ready to go to church. On this morning, I was going to go alone, and I was going to walk. The church was in the town of Roganville. I knew exactly how to go and how long it would take me to get there. I don't remember where the others in the family were that morning.

It was about a mile to the church if I stayed on the road we usually walked. But I knew a short cut through the woods that would get me there quicker. Remember, I had to cross Thickety Creek to get to town.

There is nothing smarter than a 10 year old who thinks he doesn't need instructions. Mom did not give me specific instructions to stay on the regular roads, but I knew she expected me to. So, I left home and when I reached the place where I knew there was a foot log across the creek, I knew that would cut off a lot of walking getting to town and the church.

The proper route was to walk to the main road and cross the creek on the bridge where we normally did. I left the road and began going through the woods to the creek. I knew exactly where the log was that lay across the creek. You can probably guess what happened while crossing the creek on the log. I slipped off the log, fell in the creek, and got my shoes and pants wet. I couldn't go on to church like that, so you can imagine how long the walk felt as I went back to the house.

I knew Mother would be upset when I got back home wet. Sure enough, she was mad and disappointed. What disturbed her the most was that my shoes were wet. We got only one pair of shoes per year. I won't go into what happened. You can well imagine.

The thing that stuck in my mind and hurt the most was Mother's disappointment with me. I kept telling myself for several years that I never wanted to hurt her again by acting against her desires.

A Mule and Blinders

For a short while when I was about 10 or 11, we had an old mule. I don't remember where Dad got the mule or anything else about it, but I do remember some things about using the mule.

We used him to pull a slide and haul firewood from the woods to the house to use in fireplace, the wood burning kitchen stove, and the wash pot. The slide was just a low sided box on wooden runners turned up at the front so they would move along without hanging up on things. We had to keep it on fairly smooth ground. It was OK off the dirt road as long as we didn't run into a log or a deep hole.

This old mule was as tame and docile as he could be. Like a lot of us, this mule was always looking for something to be afraid of. So, when harnessing him to something, we had to put blinders on each side of his eyes so he could not see what was beside him. This created blind spots on each side of him so he would stay focused only on things straight ahead. I wanted his goal to be to follow the trail or road we were on.

One day while roaming the woods, I found a downed hardwood treetop that would make great firewood for the stove, fireplace, and wash pot. This treetop was located too far from the house to use a wheelbarrow to bring some of the wood home. I begged Mom and Dad to let me harness the mule to the slide to haul some wood home.

After assuring them that I could handle the mule without any trouble and that I would be extra careful, I managed to get the harness on the mule and led him to where the slide was. He understood back up, go ahead, and whoa. I hooked the harness to the eye bolts on the slide, and I was ready to go. I had me a mule pulling a slide. I thought I was grown up. Mistake number one.

I got behind the slide and shook the reins while telling the mule to git up. We went down the sandy road for a while, then turned off into the woods to go to the treetop I had found. When we (me and the mule) got to the treetop, I yelled for him to whoa. He did and stood patiently, because stopping meant he could hang his head and rest. He did not much like work of any sort.

Well, soon I had the slide loaded with some great looking pieces of wood. I used a one man crosscut saw to cut it in pieces small enough to load on the slide. It was time to start home. I took the reins and told the mule to git up. He started to move and then stopped and shook his head. I could not get him to move. He was not agitated but he just would not move.

I studied the problem and decided to try and lead him holding his harness near his head. We started moving, but he would not go the direction I wanted. I knew I had to get to the reins again and guide him with the bit. I turned loose of the harness and walked back to the back of the slide where I had tied the reins. As soon as I let go of his harness, he turned toward two small trees that he could walk between, but the slide wouldn't go through. When the slide touched the trees, he stopped.

I was in a quandary; I could not back the mule up because the slide was stuck between the trees. The old mule was content to stand there. There was nothing to do but unload the slide, unhook the harness, lead the mule to a tree and tie his reins so he had to stay there. He didn't mind a bit; he was not working.

I unloaded the slide, then I could drag it back enough to get it turned so I could harness the mule to it again. I was getting super tired and worried I would be gone from the house too long and someone would come looking for me. I knew whoever it was would have a good laugh at me.

I reloaded the slide, but not as much wood as before. I took the reins and yelled at that old mule to get going. You know what he did? He leaned into the harness just enough to be sure it was not as hard to pull as it was before. So, we headed home with a slide full of wood, but not as much as I had piled on the slide at first.

Lesson learned. Animals are much smarter than a boy who thinks he is smart. Never underestimate one of God's creations.

The Town of Roganville, Texas

I grew near a small town called Roganville. It was originally established when John Henry Kirby constructed a sawmill there around 1900. When Kirby Lumber Co. built a sawmill, they also built houses for the workers and a commissary to sell food to the employees. A worker usually did not get very much money at payday. Charges for housing and commissary bill were deducted from the pay first.

Often in sawmill towns, the workers were paid in tokens that could be spent in the commissary and used to pay rent. I heard my parents talking about times like that in their past. By the time I was born, the sawmill, all the houses, and commissary were gone.

Roganville was about 5 miles from highway 96, which went from Kirbyville to Jasper. Of course, the highway went to many other towns, but my world did not include them.

As the highway approached Roganville, there was a sharp curve in the road. It was almost a 90-degree turn. It was named "Dead Man's Curve." About another mile, the road reached the center of town. There was a small store on the right named Hoeny's, which was at the top of a steep hill, with the post office on the right at the bottom of the hill. That was the center of town.

Just past the post office, the railroad tracks crossed the road. Right past the railroad tracks, there was a grocery store on the left side of the road, Sheffield's Grocery. At this point, the pavement stopped. The road continued as a dirt road. We lived a mile further on.

If we back up to the top of the hill where Hoeny's store was, there was a road that turned left. On this road was the schoolhouse and the church. Then the road turned right and came back to the main road near the post office. It was just a loop with houses on both sides.

Post Office

The post office was in W.A. Falkner's home. He built a room on the house that faced the road. In this room were the mailboxes that people rented. (Our box was number 62). The room also had a sliding window where the postmaster or post mistress would help customers. Stamps were available, packages could be sent. Most any postal transaction could be completed.

School

The school was a one room schoolhouse with grades 1 through 11 in one large room. The teacher would group students according to their grade level. I remember it being loud and noisy. It was the older kids who made a lot of noise, but they were not rude to the teacher. If a student was way out of line, their parents would be told. That was something to be dreaded. Bad behavior at school was not tolerated by parents. How they found out things was a mystery. No one had telephones, but parents seemed to know everything that went on.

I went two years to this school. I remember it being mostly play time for me. When I was in the second grade, a group of parents got together and had a meeting with the school board of Jasper. This school was part of their system. So, it was decided the one room school would close and students would ride the bus to Jasper. Parents were not all happy with the decision.

Somehow, I was transferred to Kirbyville school for one year. I think it was because of bus service. Then I started going to a middle school out on highway 96 that was called Temple Springs. It had grades 1 through 8 and was supervised by Kirbyville school district. There are good and bad memories of the time I spent at this school.

Church

The church was also a one room building. The church pews were made from wood slats that sure did get hard about halfway through a sermon. I think it was built as a Baptist church, but each Sunday of the month a different denomination met there. I went every Sunday I could. Mother saw to that. I would dream up reasons why I should not go. My mom never seemed to agree with me.

By the summertime, I would have either outgrown or worn out my shoes. I would try to use the excuse that I could not go to church barefoot. Mom said, "Well, you go to the store barefoot, and besides, most of the other kids do not have shoes either."

I went to church even if my shoes were worn out. I remember sitting on the back row of the church during the service so I could stick my feet under the pew, and no one could see I was barefoot. We each got new shoes every fall from Sears and Roebuck catalogue. I know now that many other children experienced the same thing.

Sometimes when there was someone to teach a Sunday School lesson, I went early enough to attend this. Mother seemed to know ahead of time if there would be Sunday School.

I know now the Sunday that the Baptist preacher was to be there, there was we had Sunday School. Every once in a while, the teacher would have some used books for the lesson. Those were the ones I really enjoyed. The Sunday School books had lots of pictures to go with the lesson. There were not enough books for us to take one home. I do remember wanting to have one of the books. Even as a boy, I read everything I could get.

I do not remember the ladies' names that taught Sunday School. For this, I am really sorry.

Some of My Toys

As a child living in a rural environment, there were not many bought toys. As a small boy, cars and trucks were some of my favorites.

As I said in an earlier story, I played under the house a lot. I built the roads out of soft sandy soil. I would use things like empty cans and boards to make bridges. My cars were mostly snuff bottles I would find in trash piles in the woods. Snuff bottles were square brown bottles that were good for toy cars.

Most Christmases I would get a cap pistol and holster. I would wear that everywhere I could until the holster fell apart. A few times I received a pair of pistols. Boy, that was the best. I could practice drawing one or the other or maybe both at the same time. I could pretend to be the Lone Ranger or Gene Autry and capture lots of crooks and horse thieves. If one of my friends also had a cap pistol, we could play war or team up on the outlaws.

Another neat toy was tin cans, which were excellent things to kick as we walked (if we had shoes) or to hit with a stick. (Small Carnation milk cans were the best). If there were other boys around, we played tin can shinny. I do not remember much about it except that we tried to hit the can with a stick, farther than anyone else.

As I grew a little older, I carried a sling shot in my pocket most of the time. Many times, the stock was made of a forked stick that was strong enough not to break off when pressure was put on them by strands of rubber. Sometimes I would find the end of an apple box and saw a stock out of that wood. (I found lots of treasures while roaming the woods where people would carry trash that would not burn). I mostly used strips of rubber from old automobile inner tubes I would find in these trash piles.

The slings were made of tongues from old shoes that were thrown in the trash. When a shoe was deemed worn out and thrown away, the tongue was always cut out to be used when a small piece of leather was needed.

The absolute best rubber for the slingshot strips were ones cut from a red inner tube. (I did not know at the time that they were made from natural rubber). I remember finding the old red tubes became very hard. I know now that companies were starting to use synthetic rubber to make the tubes. World War II was in full swing.

Another toy I had was a simple iron ring that I rolled with a T-shaped stick. We could roll it up hill or downhill, if the hill was not too steep. It worked best if the area was smooth. It had to be a road or a much-used trail for it to be fun. Many times, I went to town rolling the ring. When I crossed the creek bridge, I picked the ring up and carried it over the bridge. The bridge had cracks in it, so the ring could fall through. The steel rings were hard to find. The adults liked to use them as a latch for gates. I thought that was a waste of a good ring. The picture below is a modern version.

Figure 3 Trundling hoop and roll

I was not very old when I got my first pocketknife. I do not really remember my first knife, but it had to be one that my dad had already worn out. I remember being quite proud of my pocketknife. I would borrow my dad's whet rock to sharpen it. I learned to use my pocketknife constantly. It was enjoyable to sit and whittle on a stick or piece of soft wood. One of the best woods for whittling was red cedar. It has such a pleasant aroma as I cut thin slivers off of a piece. I still carry and use a pocketknife today.

Our Dogs

While I was a young boy, We had two dogs. One was a brown spotted Feist. His name was Lightning. My dad named him. As you can imagine, he did everything as fast as he could. He always seemed in a hurry.

My dad got Lightning when he was very young. He became my pet until it was time to go squirrel hunting. Then he was no one's pet. His goal was to find and tree a squirrel. Throughout the area, Lightning was well known as a great squirrel dog.

No one could borrow him for hunting, even people who had been in a hunting party previously, because as soon as they went into the woods without one of our family with the group, Lightning would leave and start towards home, even if it was ten miles away.

We had another large mixed breed Cur dog. His name was Ted. He was also a pet. He was rather old when we got him. His specialty was racoons. His ears were in shreds on the ends where he had been in fights with coons. Most of the time, he just laid around until someone went hunting.

If Ted was taken into the woods at night, he came alive. If it was near a creek or a branch, he would soon have a racoon treed, and not always in a tree. If it were near the creek, the coon would get to the center of the creek where the dog would have to swim to get near him. Ted was smart enough to know to leave the coon alone if he was in the water. Racoons have been known to drown a dog in the water.

He would also occasionally tree squirrels. Even hunting, he would back Lightning up even though Lightning seldom needed help squirrel hunting.

These two dogs were buddies. They would travel all around and even go to town. They stayed together, but when another dog appeared, Lightning would always start a fight. It did not matter if the other dog was twice his size. Invariably, a larger dog would be getting the best of Lightning, and Ted would step in and the other dog left. Ted was fierce when he had to fight.

In that time, dogs were not allowed in a house, especially a hunting dog. Our dogs were not even allowed on either the front or back porch. When it was time to eat, they might come to the steps, but never up on a porch.

A Squirrel Hunting Trip

Some men that my dad knew or had worked with asked him to take them hunting with the famous dog, Lightning. I remember at least one of the men was a lawyer from Jasper. I do not remember how old I was at the time.

Before we left the house, my dad told the men how unique Lightning was. I am sure he embellished the story. He told them to watch Lightning as soon as we reached the woods. He told them that Lightning would pick up a small stick and prance around with it in his mouth. (Lightning always did this simply because he was excited knowing we were going hunting. It was just something he did. No one had taught him to do this.)

Dad told the men that when Lightning treed the first squirrel, he would lean the stick against the tree to mark where the squirrel was. Then he would go on and tree another. Of course, the men laughed and sort of made fun.

When we got to the woods where we were going to hunt, sure enough the dog picked up a stick and went around to everyone twisting and whining with the stick in his mouth. I saw some of the men laugh and point to the dog. After we walked a little into the woods, Dad told Lightning to "go ahead." The dog took off running with the stick still in his mouth.

It was not long until we heard Lightning barking. By listening, you could tell he was staying in the same place, so we started toward his bark. When we reached the tree, sure enough there was a squirrel in the tree. Someone took the squirrel down and immediately Lightning was gone looking for another squirrel.

I looked around, sure enough, two of the men were walking around the tree looking for Lightning's stick. Dad and I had a good laugh about this later.

Another Hunting Trip

On another hunting trip, there was just me, my dad, and another person. I don't remember who it was. We had both Ted and Lightning with us.

As we were walking slowly through the woods waiting for one of the dogs to tree, we came upon a downed tree. This was a good-sized tree, and the top was still very dense with dried leaves and branches. One of the members of our party said, "I hear something in that treetop." So, we all three stopped walking and listened for any sounds coming from the treetop. Every few minutes, there was a slight rustling in the dry leaves of the treetop. None of us wanted to try and get in the dry branches to see what it was.

About that time, we heard the dogs trotting through the woods coming to us. The dogs knew that they were expected to come and check in every so often if they had not found a squirrel to tree.

Ted reached us first, trotting along slowly. He was probably bored with all this traipsing around through the woods. When he stopped, my dad tried to get Ted to go into the treetop and see what was in there. No amount of coaching or talking to the old dog convinced him to go in that tree. He would go to the edge of the branches, but then he would back up and stop. He was not going into the treetop.

About that time here comes Lightning. He did not even stop to greet anyone. He just bailed off into the thick branches of the treetop. Of all the squealing, growling, barking, and rustling around in those limbs, it sounded like a war was going on. Ted still would not put a foot in there. He just stood and barked a little.

When the bobcat finally turned Lightning loose, that dog came shooting out of the tree in a dead run and headed for home. No amount of calling slowed him down. He was still yelping at every jump. The squirrel hunt was over. The bobcat trotted off to another thicket.

When we got back home, Lightning was laying under the house licking his wounds. As it turned out, he only had a few scratches and cuts. He was fine within a few hours.

One of My Favorite Places to Spend Time

In the woods about a quarter of a mile from the house there was a large hole in the ground. In the bottom was a spring of water that started a branch that ran all the time. This was the original water source for my grandfather's house when it was built in the 1800s.

Further down this branch is where I would spend time damming the stream up and having lots of fun. This cavity in the ground was quite large. There were trees growing up from the bottom. This spring water was fresh and cool, even in hot summertime.

This place fascinated me. I would spend many hours each week just sitting at the top edge of what I called my canyon. It was a good place to sit and read or watch for squirrels, rabbits or some other creature that might come to get a drink. As I sat at the top of the "canyon," I enjoyed the smells carried in the air. The smells depended on the time of the year. In the fall there were hints of the dried leaves and sometimes the odor of animals. By sitting quietly by a tree, I would see squirrels in the trees and sometimes a feral hog would pass by going to get a drink.

In the spring, the smells were different. The yellow jasmines gave off a sweet aroma that drifted along with the breeze. The honey suckles (wild azaleas) bloomed near the branch formed by the spring in my "canyon." Their aroma was very sweet.

If I listened closely, I could hear the slight tinkle as the water ran from the spring. In fact, the only sounds were made by the wind, the water running, and the animals.

This place was in a grove of beech trees. In spring and summer, it was usually shady and cool. During the fall when the beech nuts matured, I could quietly watch the squirrels gathering the nuts. The nuts were in a cluster with each nut enclosed in a very spiny hull. It was almost impossible to get to the nut without getting little spines in the fingers. The squirrels could do it. Sometimes it sounded like rain when there were several squirrels in the trees eating the nuts. I had to be very still and quiet to hear this.

If I did not make much noise and paid attention, I could hear Mom if she called me from the house. Often, she would have to call me, because I would get lost in a book or just not paying attention to how long I had been there. It was so easy to let myself get immersed into the sights and sounds of God's creations.

There were numerous chores I was expected to do around the house, but not so many to be a burden, even for a ten- or eleven-year-old. I tried very hard to react to Mother's calls promptly. I did not want to be told I could not go to the "canyon." Many times, after we had moved to town, I wanted to go back to this place. I never got the chance.

Our Water Well

Many years before my time, someone decided they would dig a well near the house. Well, someone really must have been tired of carrying water, because they dug a well about five or six feet from the outside wall of the kitchen. The well was dug by hand. It was easy to tell that someone had dug the well with shovels.

Mother did not remember when it was dug. It was about twenty feet to the water. There was a wooden structure around it and a roof over it so nothing could fall in. There was a door from the kitchen that opened near the well.

Once the well had to be emptied because it had become contaminated. To get the well empty, there had to be two buckets on the rope that went through the well pully. While one full bucket was being raised, the empty bucket was dropping into the well to be filled. The water ran into the well so fast it was quite a job to get it empty. I was too small to help with that because it had to be done fast to draw out more water than was running into the well.

Once it was just about empty, we could look in the well and see the bottom. There was actually a stream flowing through the bottom of the well. It was obvious the well had been dug on top of an underground stream. When the well was empty, someone went down to get any debris or foreign objects out of the well. Once the well was clean and nothing was contaminating the water, the men stopped drawing water out and let it fill back up. It had to sit for a couple of days for the water to be clear enough to drink.

I have often wondered how the well was located in such an ideal place to have fresh cold water all the time. It must have been located using a divining rod. There were a few men still around who were known for their ability to use a divining rod.

I have tried to use one in forestry presentations, and it does not work for me. It works for my son Ray. I saw it at one of these presentations.

Invisible Friends

My brother, John Maston, was eight years older than me, my sister, Juanita, was 5 years older, and Robbie was not yet born. Mother stayed busy doing washing, ironing, and cooking and she did not have a lot of extra time. But when I needed her, she was always there and willing to be Mama.

When I was around six to eight years old, I must have decided I needed some friends. I created two invisible friends who I conversed with about everything. I could tell them anything I wanted. I knew they would not tell anyone.

Their names were K-K and Hoo-Hoo. I am guessing at the spelling of their names since I was not old enough to read at that time.

My mom knew their names. Many times, I remember her asking if she needed to set them a place at the table when she fixed a snack or meal just for me. Sometimes I would say yes and sometimes I told her they had eaten already. And sometimes I would say set just one place. Hoo-Hoo was gone that day.

Mom never asked anything about them during meals with the family. She never made fun of me for having invisible friends. Occasionally she would ask me if they were with me that day. I remember her smiling as she went on about whatever she was doing. I never felt that it bothered or concerned her.

I also remember talking to them while playing with my cars under the house. Or telling them not to climb a tree that I was up in. I told them they might fall. How I remember these things, I do not know.

In today's world, a child that did this might be considered mentally disturbed. Probably be taken to a Neurologist for evaluation.

I am glad I can remember this experience. I know now that God, through the Holy Spirit, had a purpose for this. One day I will ask Him why.

Purple Glass

As I roamed the woods, the old logging roads, and trails, I was always looking for unusual things. I found a few old glass bottles or drinking glasses that people had thrown away a long time before.

These glass things were clear at one time, but exposure to the sun caused them to turn purple. They would be different shades of purple, from a light lavender to a dark purple. I thought the purple glass was pretty. I would take them home to Mom.

Somehow a lady who lived in town found out about these purple glass things. She sent word that she would pay me twenty five cents each for all I could bring her. She had a collection of this type of glass. Her name was Mrs. Bethany. I became busy looking for purple glass. A quarter was big money for a ten or eleven year old boy.

Being paid for these things meant that I could buy my own soda water and peanuts. I always selected a bottle of Royal Cream Cola; it was the largest bottle in the cold drink cooler at the store. With a 5-cent bag of peanuts, I had a big treat.

When I started to write this little story, I did a little research and found that the clear glass made in the 1930's had an ingredient that would cause it to turn purple. It was called Solarized glass, and the ingredient is Manganese Dioxide.

Catching Armadillos

When I was a kid, the woods were full of armadillos. They were easy to catch. They do not see very well and do not move very fast. A person could slip up on them if they moved slowly and quietly. But if an armadillo sees or hears someone near him, he will run for a hole in the ground. Once he starts into the hole, he cannot be pulled out. He digs in with his claws and holds on tight, and even if someone has a hold on his tail, they still cannot pull him from the hole. He will not come out for quite a while.

One of the conductors on the passenger train that came through Roganville twice each week would buy live armadillos for 50 cents each. I would try to catch a couple the morning the train was coming through. I carried the armadillos in a tow sack (burlap bag) and waited for the train.

When the train stopped, the conductor would come out of the passenger car and look for anyone waiting to board the train. When he saw me with the tow sack in my hands, he would ask, "How many do you have in that sack, boy?" I would hold up two fingers, and he would reach in his pocket and hand me two fifty cent pieces.

I was elated with my money. First stop was the grocery store to get a cold soda water to drink on my way home.

Trip to Visit Mama and Papa Wright

My grandparents' names were Lena Read Wright and John Maston Wright. She was a slight-built lady with dark hair. He was a large man with reddish complexion, he was of Irish descent, and he had a mustache.

Mama and Papa Wright lived in Tyler County, Texas in a community called New Hope. It was 7 miles east of the town of Warren. The only thing that identified New Hope was the New Hope Baptist Church. It was just down the road from my grandparents' house. My uncle, Dad's brother-in-law, was the pastor of this church.

My grandparent's place was very interesting to a boy. The house had a hall down the center just like our house did.

My grandfather tanned deer hides into leather that was soft as a blanket. He also made and used leather whips. He could pop the whip loud enough to be heard a long way. He would have me stand in front of him, and he would make the whip wrap around my legs and pop, but it never touched my legs.

He used the sound of the whip to call his hogs in the evening so he could feed them. He would pop the whip a few times and, after a little while, I could hear the hogs coming. They would gather around a wooden trough, and he would put their food in it. If one of the hogs pushed against him while he was putting their food in the trough, one crack of his whip and that hog left squealing. He was not a cruel man, but animals seemed to respect him.

My grandmother was deaf as far back as I can remember. I could not talk to her, and it was strange to me. I think it must have been the first non-hearing person I was exposed to. She could talk since she had been able to hear for most of her life.

On one of our visits, she asked me to go get her some sweet gum twigs. She showed me one that she had been chewing on. She was adamant that they had to be from a sweet gum tree and just the right size. She said she brushed her teeth with them. I wondered about that but accepted it and left to find a sweet gum tree. There were plenty of woods around their house, so I soon cut a handful of twigs using my pocketknife. I made sure they were the correct size. I can remember being proud to give them to her. I remember her hugging me and saying thank you.

Years later I found out that she used the twigs to put snuff on and then chew on the twig. She dipped snuff.

When several families were there at the same time, when mealtimes came, the children did not eat until all the adults were through eating. That was just the way it was. We were not allowed in the kitchen until the adults were through.

I remember visits there when it was just our family. At mealtimes, we all sat at the dining table to eat. The places at the table were set with a fork and spoon under a plate that was turned upside down over the silverware. When everyone was seated at the table, no one turned their plates over until Papa had said the blessing and turned his plate over.

When it came bedtime, I slept on a pallet in my grandparents' room. This was also the room with the fireplace. My grandparents' bed was quite large, and the mattress was stuffed with down feathers.

Each morning, my grandfather would make the bed using a broom. He could make the bed look so smooth just using the broom. Of course, I wanted to try but always left large bumps in the bed. He would take the broom and make it smooth again. (After I was older, I wondered just how many ducks one would have to pick to get enough of the small down feathers to make a bed.)

On the mantel above the fireplace was the timepiece for the house. It was an old "gingerbread" clock made by E. Ingram Clock Co. of New Haven, Connecticut. In later years, I had the honor of repairing this clock. My younger sister still has it.

Papa told this story of how they came to have the clock. He and Mama were just married and they had no clock in the house. One day a peddler came by in his wagon with pots and pans and other things for sale. Papa said they had no money so he began to try and barter for the clock. Papa said they had very little of value, but he did have a jug of good homebrew that he had made. The peddler wanted the homebrew badly but would not trade the clock just for the jug. Papa said he had a brand-new horse blanket that he had not used. So, he threw that in the trade. The peddler still would not go for it, so Papa said we had one quarter coin in the house. That was enough for the peddler to trade the clock. That is how they came to have the clock.

I am going to tell this, though to this day I do not understand it. But I clearly remember hearing every word of this conversation.

I remember Papa, my dad, and another man sitting on Papa's front porch. I was sitting on the top step while the adults were sitting in rocking chairs.

All at once, there was a man on a horse coming down the road as fast as the horse could run. The man stopped the horse at the gate and yelled to Papa, "Come quick! So and so (I don't remember the name) has cut his foot really bad with an axe and we can't stop the bleeding." I distinctly remember Papa telling him, "Go back, I will be there in a few minutes. The bleeding should be stopped by the time you get back." I wanted to go with Papa, but he said no. Then he said this to me, "When you are old enough, I will explain it to you."

As we were going home later, I asked Mom and Dad about what I had heard and they would not talk about it.

Figure 4 John Maston Wright

Rats and the Corn Crib

There were a few things that I really looked forward to as a young child. One was going to Uncle Webster and Aunt Mae's for a visit. They lived on a farm. There were always neat things to explore with my cousin, Kenneth.

They had a barn and a smaller building that was called a corn crib. That is where Uncle Webster stored the corn he had raised and dried.

The rats also enjoyed the corn crib. The door was up off the ground to help keep the moisture down. So, one had to climb up a little to get inside the crib. There always seemed to be rats inside. There were a couple of pieces of broom handles leaning against the wall to be used as "rat sticks."

We could move a few of the dried ears of corn and, sure enough, a rat would appear. We had to swing the stick quick and straight to get the rat. It was fun to see how many we could bump on the head with the sticks.

Uncle Webster was always pleased when there were fewer rats in the corn crib.

Going to the Movies

I looked forward to going to the movies in Kirbyville, which was a town about ten miles from home.

During World War II, without electricity or a radio, my parents could not get much news of how the war was going. So, on Saturday nights, the theater would run government news reels before and after the movie. Mother and Dad wanted to see the war news. I remember some of the news reels showed bombs bursting and some film of some of the fighter planes. At the end of the newsreels, there would be a list of the number of casualties in one place or another.

The movie was usually a western with Roy Rogers or Gene Autry. Before the movie, they also showed an episode of Batman and Robin. There was always a cliff hanger with Batman and Robin. I could hardly wait to see these. The new episode started with the last scene from the previous week.

I remember my parents discussing the news reels while going home. Mother had a nephew stationed somewhere in the South Pacific. He was killed by a sniper near the end of the war.

Remembering My Family

The personalities and demeanor of my parents were so very different. But each one dealt with life with all their strength. They lived through the Great Depression when there was almost no work available. Their lives had very few comforts. But I remember many evenings during mild weather when the whole family would sit on the porch and laugh and talk about what everyone had done that day or what they were going to do the next day. There may not have been very much in the way of material things, but there was love and happiness.

Mom

My mom was a very quiet and unassuming lady. Seldom would I hear her criticize anyone. If I made some negative remark about someone, she would set me straight in a hurry and tell me something like this,

"Every person had some value. Maybe it is not visible to us, but God knows. We are not to talk bad about anyone, because we do not know what they are going through. Treat everyone as you want to be treated."

Some of these conservations come back to me when I find myself wanting to criticize someone. Now that I have a relationship with Jesus, the Holy Spirit will convict me immediately if I start to talk bad about anyone. This seed was planted long ago by my mother.

Mother never used any type of profanity. About the strongest words I remember hearing from her was "oh fiddlesticks." If she heard me saying any word of profanity, it was very likely my mouth would get washed out with lye soap.

I think I learned patience and compassion for others from her. She never seemed to get upset and criticize other people.

Mom was taken early in life at sixty-six years of age. I still tell myself today that God took her so she could rest and live in joy with Jesus. I will see her again one day.

Figure 5 My Mom

Dad

My dad was a very outdoor person. He lived to fish and hunt. He would work at most any job to feed our family. Those days were not like today where we try to save a certain portion of our income. Money was not saved, simply because there never seemed to be enough to pay the grocery bill and buy a few new clothes for everyone.

He taught me to try and do the best I could when making something or working to repair something. He was an excellent auto mechanic. I guess he learned it by doing it. I learned some things by handing him a wrench or socket he needed while at work on an auto. He would also take time to explain to me about the repairs he was doing. Many times, when he was under an old car working, I would lie down at the edge so he could tell me what tool he needed. He could be rather impatient if I was too slow to find the proper tool.

One thing he did that I really did not like was his choice of words. He used too many curse words. Later in life he stopped that. That was a blessing.

His siblings treated him like a black sheep. Many times, there were gatherings at his parents, and he was not notified. I know it hurt his feelings even though he never complained. He would just say something like, "I did not have time to go anyway." Which was not true. I know he and Mom talked about this, but always in private.

In those times, children were not included in things they should not have been. If there was something you needed to know, you were told. Otherwise, you did not listen to adult's conversations. From this, I learned not to walk up to folks when they were engrossed in conversation. I was taught to respect other's space.

I did learn how to fish and squirrel hunt from Dad. The only problem I had was he was so intent on fishing or hunting that some trips never seemed to end. He never got tired of trying. Because of his persistence, he most always caught more fish than others. Persistence was another lesson even though I did not know I was learning it.

I learned how to sharpen knives, how to safely use an axe, crosscut saw, a pole peeler, a pocketknife, and many other little things.

My dad lived to be eighty-two. When I asked him about eternal life, he told me he knew Jesus.

My Older Brother

I was blessed with one older brother and two sisters, one older and one younger.

My brother was born September 20, 1929. He was the only one of my siblings born in a hospital. He was born in Woodville, Texas. He was named John Maston Wright after our grandfather. He grew up being a constant companion of my father. As soon as he was old enough, he hunted and fished with my dad. He grew up to be course and rough on the outside, but he had a great heart for his younger siblings. He and my older sister were super close as they grew up.

When he reached his teenage years, he was quite mischievous. In those days, it was a big thing on Halloween to irritate the townspeople by doing things like turning the gate of a yard fence around backwards or hiding the gate somewhere close. Hurricane fencing was a novelty in those times, so it made a good target for Halloween mischief.

John Maston and some of his friends would have a fried chicken cookout sometimes at night. The problem was that the chickens came from someone's chicken house without their knowledge. It is a wonder some of them did not get shot. People knew who was getting their chickens, they just could not catch them. Sometimes the teen boys would take the farmers' fish or game they had harvested. No one asked why.

After high school, John Maston worked in sawmills and sometimes for the electric co-op. At one time, he had an Indian motorcycle. He mostly drove an old stripped-down car without a top because he and his friends chopped it off with an axe.

Late at night, if he was coming through town, He would stop in the center of town and yell at the top of his lungs. He could be heard for a quarter of a mile. He did it simply to irritate the townspeople.

He was drafted in the army at about nineteen years old. He never went overseas but spent most of his time in the northeast. He married and lived in Maryland and West Virginia most of his life.

Figure 6 John Maston

My Older Sister

My older sister was born June 1, 1932. I am not sure where my parents were living at that time. She was born at home with a midwife and a doctor from town. She was named Francis Juanita Wright.

She was five years older than me. My memories of her as a child are vague, but when I remember things about her, it was her helping mother in the kitchen and house. By that time, she was a young teen. We walked to school together when I was in the first and second grades. It was a one room schoolhouse with all grades in the same room. She would fuss at me if I stepped in a mudhole or anything that would dirty my shoes.

When she was an older teen, I think I must have aggravated her quite a bit. She did not want me in her room. She would yell for Mom if I tried to sneak in. I would go under the house to where her room was above me and beat on the floor with a stick or do anything else I could to bother her when she was studying or reading. At about thirteen years old, she started attending school in Kirbyville. We both rode the school bus. I went to a school that was first through the eighth grades. I was in the third grade.

After she graduated from high school, she worked for the electric co-op in their office in Kirbyville. She later went to Beaumont and worked as a church secretary for Magnolia Avenue Baptist Church.

Later, she married Mike Husbands. He was born and raised in Kirbyville. I do not know if they knew each other in high school.

They were one of the most dedicated and compatible couples I ever knew. They were both strong Christian believers and spent their lives serving God and the church. They had two daughters, Melanie, and Melissa and lived most of their lives in Buna, Texas. They served in the First Baptist Church there until they could not do anything. Their lives were dedicated to God's work. Their next love was the public library in Buna. They served there faithfully and became the managers of the library and its funds.

Figure 7 Juanita and Me

My Younger Sister

Robbie Lea Wright was born August 18, 1945. She was born at home with a midwife (Mrs. Renfro) and Dr.

McWright who came from Kirbyville. I was almost eight years old when she was born.

Unlike the world today, I have no memory whatsoever of my mother being pregnant. I have tried to find some memory that would have told me she was expecting a baby. In those days, that was never talked about around children. I do remember that I was awakened by someone, and Dad told me I had to go to Mrs. Renfro's house for the night. There were several people in our house, but I don't remember who they were.

I do not remember there being a baby in the house. Obviously, there was, because I later remember having a little sister around.

Robbie was seven or eight years old when we moved to town. After high school, she attended a business school in Beaumont. She married Byron Kollenborn, who was in the military. They lived all around the world until he retired as an officer in the army.

Byron and Robbie have two children. Robin and Keith.

Figure 8 Me holding Robbie with Lightning at our feet

The Coming of Spring

Every year, I wished spring and warm weather would hurry. As I walked around in the outdoors, I would look at the Beech and other trees that were bare of leaves and think how pretty they would be when the new green leaves began coming out. The new leaves seemed almost like velvet to the touch. I would complain to Mom, and she would just say, "Don't wish your life away, son. Go read a book or gather some more wood for the fireplace or the stove."

As we began to have days when the sun felt warm if I could get out of the cold wind, I would find me a tree large enough to block the wind but let me still sit in the sun. It felt so good with the warm sun shining on me.

I would soon tire of sitting still and would roam around looking for anything that indicated spring. One of the first signs of spring was Wild Violets blooming. These were large blooms and so delicate and pretty. I liked them because they were on of my mom's favorite flowers.

Sometimes I would try and dig one up and replant it near the house. Most of the time they never lived.

Soon after the Violets, the Yellow Jasmine vines (Carolina Jasmine) would begin to bloom. Sometimes on a calm day or a day with a light breeze, I could smell the aroma before I saw the flowers. I think this was one of my favorite wildflowers.

Another flower that bloomed in the early spring was a plant we called Honeysuckle. After I was grown, I learned the correct name was Wild Azalea. They are a light pink, very delicate flower with an amazing aroma. They grow in moist areas of the east Texas outdoors near branches and creeks.

As the weather warmed, I wanted to go barefoot. Mom watched closely to be sure I wore my shoes until it was warm enough. As soon as I could go barefoot, I could wade in the edge of the creek and in the branches that were from a couple of springs I knew about.

There were times when I would slip off my shoes and wade, then dry my feet as best I could and go back to the house with my shoes on. Mother seemed to always know. She would ask me if I had been dabbling in the branch without my shoes.

Sliding Down a Hill

O n the east side of the house a couple of hundred yards away, there was a tall growth of pine trees that were quite large. They were thick and grew tall with no underbrush growing because they blocked most of the sunshine from reaching the ground. Over the years, the pine trees dropping their needles created a carpet of pine needles that was very smooth.

This stand of trees grew on a hill that was steep, sloping down to a small branch of water. It was fun to slide down the slope on the carpet of pine straw. But, being kids, we wanted something more than this. We looked for ways to make the sliding better and faster.

We found some wooden staves from old nail kegs. These boards had a slight curve to them. We immediately thought if we could make them smooth, we could use them like skis. No thoughts whether someone might fall and hit a tree.

We started working on the outside of the curved side of the boards. We did not have things like sandpaper so we used rocks or whatever old tool might make the boards smooth. We found a little bit of sandpaper and an old wood rasp and rubbed and sanded and polished with rocks until they were very smooth.

Then we would get at the top of the hill and squat on the backends of two of the staves and push off to slide down the hill. What we found out soon enough was that the more we used the boards, the smoother they became and the faster we went.

For some time, we would play on the hill and, of course, a few times someone would try to stand up on the boards and run into a tree. A few skinned places, but we and our friends had fun.

Here is a picture of a nail keg so you can get an idea of what we were using. The Keg staves were about 2 feet long.

Learning to Drive

I learned to drive in little bits. If Dad needed the car moved from one place to another, he would tell me, "Go get the car and bring it here." So, I would go crank the car and move it where he wanted. I mostly learned by watching him.

I learned to actually "drive" in a 1941 ford that the metal body had been removed. Someone had built a complete pickup body using plywood and lumber. I have mentioned this vehicle before.

I would drive a short distance down one of the dirt roads and turn around and drive back to the house. But I could not do this very often because of the availability of gasoline.

I had never really driven anywhere until one time when we made a trip to Papa Wright's house near Warren. There was to be a gathering of Dad's siblings at Papa's house one weekend. I do not know how Mom and Dad found out about it, because none of his siblings had contacted him or Mom. I knew this from hearing Mom and Dad discuss it.

It seems Dad was sort of outlawed by his brother and sisters, they thought he was not up to the same standard as they were, except for one sister. She enjoyed fishing as much as he did. His brother and older sister thought he was irresponsible and enjoyed getting together without him. At any rate, Dad decided we were going. Mom tried to talk him out of it, but he insisted.

We started out normally, but instead of going the route across the Neches River at Sheffield's ferry and through Spurger, we started down the road toward Silsbee. I knew going in that direction that we did not have to cross the river on a ferry. There was a river bridge in Silsbee. It was longer this way, but that was OK with me. I liked to ride in the car, which I think was a 1937 or 1939 Ford sedan.

After Silsbee, we drove on highway 92 to Fred. In Fred, we turned onto a dirt road that ended at the New Hope Church a short distance from Papa's house.

On this road, we had to cross a couple of bridges over some creeks. One was Thuvenin's Creek. When we came to this creek bridge, Dad stopped the car just before the bridge and proceeded to get out of the car. Mom said, "John what are you doing?" Dad said he was going to fish along the creek, and he would see us at Papa's. The creek ran within a quarter of a mile of Papa's house.

Then Dad said, "Boy, get up here and drive on to Papa's. Just don't hit a tree." I was maybe ten or eleven years old. It was about five miles to Papa's house.

We made it with no issues. Mom was upset at first but was laughing about it by the time we got to the house. After that, I felt like I could drive.

This story would not be finished without noting the reactions of the folks at Papa's house. His father just laughed about it and said we would have a mess of fish. His brother and older sister acted as if someone had done something to them.

They were upset that we had come and even more upset when they knew he would get here after fishing. They were pretty dressed up.

It was getting on toward dinner time (lunch) and I could smell the sweet aromas of some tasty food coming down the hall from the kitchen.

After about an hour or so, here comes Dad walking across an old field towards the house. He was wet and dirty and carrying a string of bass. His older sister would not speak to him. I remember him smiling with happiness at their reactions. He told me in front of everyone, "Thanks for driving the car here." Of course, I was proud as punch.

The day went over very well. In spite of what my aunts or uncle felt, they knew better than to start arguing in front of my grandfather. They all watched their speech around him.

On the ride home, everyone seemed very happy.

Blackberry Picking

Most all our jelly and jams were made by my mom. We picked dewberries and blackberries as they ripened each spring. Dewberries were the first to start getting ripe. They grew mostly on a vining briar. They were usually low to the ground or sometimes climbing up small trees or bushes. They were pretty easy to pick, but we had to watch for snakes under the berry vines.

One of my jobs was to have them located and know when they were getting ripe. It was easy to tell where there would be large amounts of berries by the white blooms that came out while it was still cool.

I would scout around for big patches of berry blooms as I started getting out in the woods as the weather warmed up in the spring.

Berry picking was an important activity for Mom and us kids. She could pick more berries than any of us. We were not supposed to be eating the berries as we picked them. We had to gather enough berries to make jelly for the whole year. Also, Mother canned a lot of berries for making cobblers.

We went berry picking very often after school and on Saturdays as long as they were ripe. Sometimes Mom would go berry picking alone while we were at school.

One day, Mom was out picking berries alone. She had called our dog Lightning to go with her. He always liked to go in the woods, but most of the time he would run off and tree a squirrel. This one day he stayed right with Mom as she went from one patch of briars to another patch, picking berries.

She approached one large clump of berry vines that were thick and tall. The dog did not want her to go up to this patch of briars. She saw a lot of nice big berries and kept trying to reach them. Finally, the dog got between her and the batch of briars and began pushing against her legs to make her back up. He finally caught her dress tail and began pulling her away from this patch. (Mother might wear a pair of pants for this type of activity, but she always wore her dress over the pants.) When it finally dawned on her what Lightning was trying to do, she left that place and told us not to go there to pick berries.

Maybe it was nothing, but any kind of varmint could have been hiding in those briars. There were plenty of bobcats in those woods.

Finding a Bee Tree

Honeybees are super important to farmers and to the people who grow family gardens. We think of bees being in a hive and attended to by someone called a beekeeper.

Bees are abundant in the wild also. Swarms of bees escape from farmers who have hives and sometimes the swarms will find a tree with a hollow in it and build a colony in the tree.

When I was a youngster, we did see bees in the woods at times. They would be on the spring flower blooms like the yellow jasmine. Occasionally, my dad or older brother would find a bee colony in a tree or stump in the woods while they were hunting. They would try and get some of the honey to bring home.

There were two distinct types of bees in our area. The large European honeybee was not very aggressive, and some of the honey could usually be "robbed." There was also a small black bee that would make colonies in trees. These bees were angry all the time. They would sting someone just for walking near their colony. Their honey could not be "robbed," even with a smoker.

I was about 10 years old the first time my dad asked me to go find a bee tree in a certain area of the woods. Dad had seen some bees while hunting, and he told me where to look for the bee tree by describing the area where he thought it was.

We identified different parts of the woods around our house by particularly different trees. It could be an old tree with limbs shaped in a certain way or maybe the tree was leaning a certain way. t could be at the top of a particular hill and sometimes by the edge of an old logging road that had been abandoned long ago. An area might have several of the same variety of trees together.

There was one area that had several beech trees growing on top of a small hill. It was called the beech hammock. I do not know why. With these descriptions, it was easy for me to find a certain spot in the woods. I asked how I would find one tree among many trees with a bee colony in it. Dad said, "Ask your mother."

I asked Mom how to find the bee tree. She laughed and handed me a jar lid with some syrup in it. Her instructions were to go to the area Dad said he thought the tree might be. Then, find a stump or a log and put the lid down and sit quietly nearby and wait for a bee to come to the syrup. If there was a tree around, a bee would soon appear. After the bee had eaten some of the syrup, the bee would fly away. I was to watch closely and follow the direction the bee flew in. When the bee flew out of my vision, I was to mark that spot in my mind and take my syrup and lid there and wait again.

Sure enough, it was not long until one lone honeybee landed on the syrup lid. In a minute or so, the bee took off. I watched as hard as I could to see which way he flew. I knew bees flew in a straight line when going back to their colony.

When the bee flew out of my vision, I walked straight to that spot, then continued walking about a hundred yards farther in the same direction. I set down my lid with syrup in it and waited on another bee. Sure enough, it was not very long until another came. When she left, it was in the same direction as the other bee had flown. I watched that bee and repeated the steps over again.

After about the fourth time, more than one bee came to my syrup lid. Only this time the bees flew back toward where I had last stopped. I knew I had passed the bee tree. I watched a few bees leave and they all were going toward this large old oak tree. I went near the oak tree and set my lid down and waited. Within minutes, there were lots of bees around the lid. I sat and watched them fly up in that tree.

Finally, after moving to see better, I could see the bees going in and out of a hole in the tree. I knew I had found the bee tree. I only had my pocketknife with me, and it was not large enough to mark the tree. I was sure I could find it again. Just to be sure, I drug a large limb and leaned it against the tree and piled other limbs around the base of the tree to make sure it would stand out when I brought Dad to show him the tree. I tried to mark it with limbs so I could just describe it and not have to come back. I did not like bees.

I went to get the jar lid, but it was covered in bees, so I decided it was best left right there. Some days later when Dad and my brother were ready, I led them straight to the tree. It was only about three fourths of a mile from the house. I stayed back away from the swarming bees while Dad and my brother cut into the tree and gathered a very large bucket of honey and comb. They laughed at me and called me a sissy. That was alright with me. I did not get a bee sting.

School Bus Wreck

While I was attending Temple Springs School, a middle school located on highway 96 about 7 miles from Roganville, I rode a school bus there and back.

The highway from highway 96 has a severe curve about one half mile before getting into town. It was nicknamed Dead Man's Curve. I mentioned this in the earlier description of the town of Roganville.

Coming home from school one afternoon, I was sitting on the first bench behind the bus driver. I enjoyed sitting there because I could see the road ahead. It was fortunate that I was sitting there that day. This seat had a bar between the passenger and the back of the driver's seat. I could lean on the bar while I watched the road.

There was a gentleman from Kirbyville (or Jasper) who brought newspapers to Roganville each day. For some reason, he was late that day. Just as the bus was entering Dead Man's Curve, the newspaper man was driving so fast he had to cut the curve to be able to make it around. That put him in the same lane as the bus. I remember grabbing the bar in front of me and holding on tight as the car collided head-on with the bus.

The school buses of that era had bench seats running from front to back. After the impact, kids were piled up on top of one another toward the front of the bus. Of all the screaming, crying, and yelling, people were trying to get up at the same time and were having difficulty. Everyone was tangled up and some had injuries. It was pandemonium to say the least.

I was fortunate not to have an injury. My arm hurt where it hit against the bar in front of me, but there was no blood on me. I remember looking to see if I was bleeding anywhere.

Cars began stopping and helping children get to the side of the road and then sitting them on the grassy side of the highway. Then parents started coming from town to check on their children. Word spread quickly. I am not sure how since there were few telephones, but cars by the bunches started arriving. My dad was one of the first ones there. He must have been in town at the post office.

There were some injuries, like fractured arms and bruises and skinned places, but no life-threatening injuries. We were blessed.

Good and Bad Times
at Middle School

I did not think about writing about my time in middle school, which we called Jr. High School, until one of my children asked if I was ever in trouble in school.

I attended a school called Temple Springs Junior High School. It was located on highway 96 about 7 miles from Roganville. I attended there from third grade through eighth grade. Then I went on to Kirbyville High school.

Some of my memories of this time are sparse. The main thing I remember is that much of it was not a happy time for me. I was extremely shy, so it was hard to interact with others, whether adults or youth. My most vivid memories are the good things that happened.

I have often wondered through the years why things were like they were. Almost every day when I got off the bus at school, there was a boy there who would try to get me to fight. Most days he took my lunch and emptied it out on the grass and laughed at what was in it. If I happened to have money to eat in the cafeteria that day, which was seldom, someone would take it. On the days I got to keep my lunch, I would hide it somewhere until lunch time. I know now that this boy probably had a bad home life and really needed someone to guide him.

I concentrated my time and efforts on trying to learn and read everything I could find. As the years went on, I worked hard to be the best student I could. In arithmetic (math) class, we learned to recite multiplication tables. Each week the teacher would have us get in line around the edge of the room. Since my last name started with a W, I was always near the end of the line to start. My goal was to be at the head of the line by the end of this exercise. Each time an answer was missed, the student went to the end of the line. I did not miss many, so a lot of days, I was near the head of the line when we finished. The next time we did the exercise, we were supposed to remember where we were in line. I tried hard to stay at the head of the line. We also did this in Spelling. I did not do quite as well.

I read every book I could check out of the library. In the seventh and eighth grades, I read all the books in the school's library. One of my teachers, Mrs. Fraley, would bring me books from Jasper Library. I never ran out of something to read. I will always be grateful for her caring. She was a real blessing to me.

In the seventh and eighth grades, I did get to play basketball, and I tried to participate in track. I was not very fast but was tall so I could high jump some. I enjoyed the time I was on our little basketball team. My dad would sometimes come and watch a game.

As for getting into trouble, it was usually because I was talking when I was not supposed to. I also got in trouble for writing and passing notes, mostly to girls. They would giggle at words I used, and the teacher would figure it out. Because I read a lot, some of the words I used were strange to them. I tried to use words they would not know on purpose. They really were not friends, just classmates.

I received a few licks with a paddle every once in a while. One time a teacher kept telling me to be still in my desk seat. I guess I was twisting and turning, which was distracting to the class. What the teacher did not know was I had a boil on my behind. I was not about to tell anyone that. So finally, when I would not sit still, the teacher gave me two licks with her paddle. She never knew, but that fixed the boil. It was drained after the paddling.

I made sure that, as best I could, my parents never knew I had received a paddling at school. I probably would have gotten another at home. In those days children were supposed to behave when at school or suffer when they came home.

My dearest friend was a boy named Clyde Kirbow. We were friends and classmates until we graduated from high school. We are close friends today. We are both in our eighties and still talk about things we did while growing up.

Occasionally we would get to spend a night together. When my paternal grandfather would come to our house for visits, Clyde would beg his parents to let him stay the night at our house. We would sit around the fireplace while Papa Wright told us stories of his childhood and other events in his life. Clyde still mentions this when we have a chance to get together.

Clyde was instrumental in my getting an interview for employment at the DuPont plant where I worked for thirty-six years. Clyde married Pat Harris, the first and only girl he ever dated.

I do not mean to imply that all was bad at Temple Springs School, it was not. These are just some of the memories that stayed with me. I made many friends through those years at Temple Springs. I did not realize it until we were all in high school. When I started high school, we had moved from Roganville to Kirbyville the summer before. We were living within walking distance to the high school.

On my very first day attending Kirbyville High School, I was confronted outside the building when I got off the school bus by the same boy who had bullied me so much at Temple Springs.

When he started to reach for my shirt collar, I punched him with my fist as hard as I could. When he got up, he walked off and never bothered me again during the four years of high school.

Another Trip to Papa and Mama Wrights

My paternal grandparents lived in New Hope Texas. This was a community about seven miles west of Warren in East Texas. This was always a fun trip for a boy.

The shortest way to get to their house was a road that ran from Magnolia Springs and Mount Union across the river to Spurger. The only unusual thing was that to get across the Neches River, we had to ride a ferry boat at a place called Sheffield's Ferry. The ferry boat had no engine. Its power came from humans. The ferry boat had a ramp on each end of the flat-bottomed boat. The ramps were lowered enough for them to sit flat on the bank of the river when the ferry was docked on either side of the river. This enabled cars to drive off or on the ferry when it was parked.

The ferry was held in place in the river by cables connected to trees on either side of the river. The cable kept the ferry from floating down the river with the current. There were rollers on the cables that were connected to the ferry. As the ferry moved along the cable, the rollers would screech and groan, making all sorts of noise. Sometimes the ferry attendant would wipe some oil from a bucket on the rollers to quieten them.

The ferry was pulled across the river by the attendant who used a wooden pole with a notch in it to lay it on the cable and literally pull the boat across the river by walking from one end of the boat to the other. He would walk to one end of the ferry, hook the pole on the cable and walk toward the other end of the boat pulling the ferry across toward the landing on the other side.

To get the car on the ferry, it had to be driven down the sloping bank of the river onto the ferry boat. That was scary. Sometimes when it had been raining quite a bit, Dad would make us get out of the car so if the car slid into the river, we would not be in it. It never slid into the river.

On occasions when the old car we had did not have very dependable brakes, Dad would also make us walk down the hill to the ferry so if he could not stop on the ferry, we would be safe on the ground. (Cars in the late thirties and early forties had mechanical brakes that did not stop the car very well.) The car also never ran off the ferry.

Once the ferry boat had traversed the river, the car had to be driven up the hill off the boat. If conditions were wet, Dad would back the car as far back on the ferry as he could, then go as fast as the car would go to get to the top of the riverbank and back on the road. Some of these rides were wild, but we always made it to the top of the hill and continued on to my grandparents' house.

Here is an actual picture of the ferry with a car on it.

Figure 9 This is the ferry that took us across the river

Hog Butchering Day

Each year in the wintertime, there was a day set aside for butchering a hog. The hog had been penned up and fed very well to fatten it up. The day selected for doing this chore was one pf the coldest and most uncomfortable days you can imagine. Ideal weather for hog butchering was near freezing temperatures, with maybe a little misting rain and no sunshine. The main reason was because there was no electricity for refrigeration. There were no stores that sold ice like we have today. So, the meat was kept cold because it was cold outside. Usually in the thirties.

There were usually neighbors who came that morning to help. This was a pretty intense day of work for a number of people. When it was time for others to butcher a hog, Dad would go help them. It was known without saying anything that the folks who came to help would go home with a package of fresh meat.

I was awakened early before any of the activities began. One of my jobs was to gather wood to burn under the washpot so there would be a big pot of hot water. The pot was also used on wash day to heat water for laundry.

I put on as many clothes as was possible and still be able to haul wood in a wheelbarrow. The wood was stacked around the other side of the house from where the butchering took place.

The cast iron washpot had to be full of water. The water was drawn from the well one bucket at a time. I would draw some water for the pot before Dad built the fire under the pot. The pot had to have water in it, or the heat might cause it to crack. Thank goodness the washpot was near the well, so I could draw a bucket and reach the pot without transferring the water to another bucket.

The water needed to be hot before other adults arrived. Dad was always telling me to hurry and get that water boiling. There was an opened top fifty-five-gallon drum set at an angle in an indention in the ground. It needed to be like this so the hog could be slid into the drum when filled with hot water.

Then after the hog was killed, it was put in the drum of hot water so the hair could be scraped off. The drum of water was at a slant so the hog could be slid in and out of the hot water. The water had to be very hot but not boiling. Water that was too hot would not allow the hair to be scraped off. It's the same if it was too cold. There were usually one or two of the men who knew exactly how hot the water should be. Most all the men would dip the tip of a finger into the water and say if they thought it was the correct temperature.

All through this I was trying to stay warm, keep the fire under the pot going, and stay ahead of what Dad wanted.

After the hog was clean inside and out, the large dining table was brought out of the kitchen and put in the yard to lay the hog on so it could be cut up.

This took me farther away from the washpot and the warm fire under it. Someone was always needing me to bring them something.

About this time, I usually was sent to the creek bottom to gather some bear grass to use for hanging the meat in the smokehouse. It was sill miserably cold and damp outside, and I sure did not enjoy that walk to get the bear grass. When I came back, if I could catch Mother when she was not real busy in the kitchen, I could get a hug and stand by the kitchen stove and warm up. Soon though, someone would call and need something brought to them.

After a time, the hog was cut up. Most of the meat was salted down in big crock containers. This was the first step to curing the meat. After a few days, the hams and shoulders would be hung in the smokehouse to begin curing. The neighbors had all gone home with a "mess" of fresh meat and Mother was cooking something that smelled great to a hungry boy.

The first things that were cooked were the liver, sliced and fried, and some of the ribs fried. Of course, there were fresh biscuits and homemade cane syrup to eat with the fried pork.

There was enough water left in the washpot to warm up some bath water. A bath felt so good and helped me feel warm.

The day after butchering was also busy. These things were always scheduled on the weekend since no one worked or went to school for two days. There was sausage to make and cracklings to cook in the washpot.

So, the next morning, once again I had to haul more firewood to the washpot. Mother would put all the little pieces of the hog that was too fat to eat in the pot to fry and render the grease out of it. This fat was used in cooking and in making lye soap. The cracklings were good to eat and Mother often made crackling cornbread.

My efforts in tending the fire around the pot for rendering the fat was a little more tedious. Building and maintaining the fire around the pot until it was hot enough to start cooking had to be done carefully. The wood had to be added slowly and gently so ashes did not fly around and get in the cracklings. Mother would stir the cracklings with a stick of wood that had been washed clean.

On this day, the sausage that was not stuffed into casings was fried and layered with some of the grease in crock containers. This preserved them for some time. (By the time we had eaten all the pan sausage, it was getting sort of rancid but not spoiled.) The sausages that were stuffed in casings were hung in the smokehouse to cure slowly in the hickory smoke. The fire in the smokehouse was very small and mostly smoldering wood to create smoke. It had to be cared for very carefully.

Some of the pork was layered in salt to preserve it. Mother used this for seasoning when cooking.

It was not too many days later that Mother made lye soap. I had to keep her with plenty of firewood for use under the washpot. I do not remember just how she made the soap. I know she used lye and grease that had been rendered when making the cracklings from the hog. The lye would burn if it got on my skin. The soap was used to wash laundry and most anything else that needed washing.

Sometimes, it was used as bath soap, but it was not very gentle on my skin,

Trouble at the Swimming Hole

We had two swimming holes near the town of Roganville. My friend and I wanted to go swimming, but it was a Saturday afternoon, and we knew the older teenagers would be there with their girlfriends. They never allowed us younger boys to swim when they were there.

My friend and I had a huddle and were trying to figure out how we could get back at them. My friend, Charles Brasher, was a couple of years younger than I, but we were fast friends and spent a lot of time together. He had an older brother, Don, who liked to cause havoc anytime. We consulted him about our problem with the older boys not allowing us to swim when they were there sparking with their girlfriends. We thought he might help us since he did not have a girl at that time. One of the older boys had stolen his girl.

Don had an old Model A Ford pickup. It was a ragged old thing, but it would run most of the time. Charles and I really liked it when Don let us ride with him around Roganville. So, Charles and I went to town to look for Don and his old pickup. We saw him and flagged him down. He considered us too young to associate with, but when we told him our problem, he seemed willing to help since he was on the outs with some of the older teens.

We climbed into the old truck and Don said we could ride around and maybe we could think of something to do about our problem with the swimming hole. We had been riding a little while and Don stopped the truck. "I know how we can have some fun with that bunch of no-good guys." Charles and I were super interested to find out what Don was thinking. He had quite a smirk on his face. He could be quite mean.

Charles and I were sort of worried, because we did not want anyone to get hurt. I knew Dad would come down on me hard if I was involved in something that could hurt someone. Don sat in the truck and told us to crank the motor. We cranked the old truck, which was quite a chore in itself. It had to be hand cranked. When it was running, Don headed the old truck back to his and Charles' house. He stopped and told us to stay there while he went to an outbuilding. He came out with a roll of electrical wire.

Charles and I just looked at each other. We did not have a clue what he was up to. We certainly did not want to really hurt someone. We told Don that we did not want to do it anymore. He assured us no one was going to be hurt.

Basically, his plan was to go to the swimming hole when the teens and girlfriends were not there. He said we would have to wait until next Saturday to do anything, but we had to get ready before then.

One evening when no one was at the swimming hole, we drove down to the creek. Charles and I had our bicycles in the truck. Don told us that when we got through, Charles and I would have to find our own way back to town.

We got out of the truck and Don got the piece of wire out of the truck. He began to drag one end of it down to one end the swimming hole where he could hide the wire and it still be in the water. The swimming hole was in a bend in the creek with a high bank on the other side. Because it was in a bend in the creek, the water moved very slowly but was cold and refreshing during the summer. Don hid the wire in the bushes near the edge of where cars were parked. Charles and I still did not know what Don had in mid.

Charles and I got our bikes out of the old truck and headed back to town. We were still not sure what Don had in mind. But we believed whatever Don had planned would give us some laughter toward the older teens.

The next Saturday rolled around, and it was a beautiful day for swimming. Hot and dry. I met Charles where we had planned, and we rode our bikes down toward the swimming hole. Don was supposed to meet us there. We eased up close enough to the creek to see that a bunch of teen boys and girls were in the swimming hole.

In a few minutes, we heard Don's old truck coming. He stopped and Charles and I hid our bikes in the bushes and climbed into the truck. He eased the truck on down to where we had planned. The teens in the swimming hole began yelling at us to leave. Don yelled back that he would leave as soon as he could get the truck going again. He jumped out of the truck and opened one side of the pieces that covered the engine. While appearing to be working on the motor, he connected the wire we had left there to a couple of the spark plugs on the old truck. Then He jumped around and cranked the truck and jumped back in it and revved up the old engine.

I have never heard so much commotion. Girls screaming, boys shouting bad words and yelling loudly. Everyone was trying to get out of the water at the same time. The magneto on that old engine put out a hefty amount of voltage with no amps. We jerked the wire loose and took off up the road with the older boys coming out of the water running toward where the truck had been. The girls were getting mad because the boys had left them to get themselves out of the water. I think maybe some couples broke up after that day.

They never saw Charles and me, so we were in the clear. We trotted to our bikes and left by another trail we knew. We went to Ferguson's store and had a soda water. I had two nickels left from selling some armadillos to the train conductor.

Sunday Afternoon Mischief

I was eleven or twelve years old at this time. Think back and try to remember how busy you wanted to be at that age.

Sunday afternoons were sort of quiet. I had been to church, came home, and we had eaten dinner (lunch). Mother was usually sitting in a rocking chair with her crochet needles working on something.

On Sunday afternoons, there was not much going on that was considered as work. It was really a day of rest for everyone. I did not think I needed to rest and be still. Sometimes on these quite afternoons, I would go find my favorite tree to sit and I would lean back against it to read a book.

This Sunday I noticed that Dad had left. I asked Mother where he was. She said he had gone to town. She did not know why. I think now she did not want to tell me where Dad really went.

I had an idea. Not always a good thing. I asked Mother if I could ride my bike to town and see if Charles was home. She said, "OK, but be careful and do not go play around the creek bridge." She knew the things I liked to do that were off limits.

I headed out to town. What I really had on my mind was to find out where Dad and my older brother were. They were both at home earlier.

When I reached the creek bridge, I stopped and looked around for any sign of cars anywhere in sight, and I did not see any. I continued toward town, looking all around as I rode across the mill yard. No car to be seen. I rode on to the post office and no one was around. There were most always men around the post office or sitting on the bench in front of Ferguson's store.

I took a road that skirted the mill yard. There was a group of pine saplings that were fairly high and a sort of a trail or road leading into them. It was evident that vehicles had been driven into the growth pine saplings. I knew that once I went into the stand of trees, there was no underbrush, and the ground was covered with pine needles.

As I came closer to the trees, I could see sort of inside the trees. It looked like Dad's car. So, I eased my way into the trees, and it really was Dad's car. There were other vehicles parked in the trees also.

I could hear the men talking and laughing. They really sounded like they were having fun. I wanted to know what was going on.

I parked my bike and walked a little further into the trees. There the men sat around a quilt spread out with money and cards scattered in front of them.

I took a couple more steps, and they all went yelling and running through the trees. Cards were scattered all around. Someone yelled "Get the pot." I saw someone grab the money (pot) and start running. I stood there wondering what all the fuss was about.

About that time, my dad saw who it was. He wanted to know what in the world I was doing there. He said it more explicitly than that. I said I just wanted to see where he was. By that time, the men were coming back trying to get their game back together. There was a lot of laughter among them. I was cautioned not to tell anyone what I saw. I did not know why, but it was fine with me.

My dad walked over to me and told me in definite words to get my butt back on that bicycle and to get out of there. He told me I had no business being there. I still did not understand what all the carrying on was about.

I think now that gambling was probably illegal in Texas in that time.

I left on my bike thankful that Dad did not yell worse than he did.

I headed down to the train yard to see if there were any new cars parked there. Sometimes there were boxcar pulpwood cars for the pulp wood cutters to load. It was always fun to climb on them or let the air off the brake system. It made quite a noise. I also would climb on the ends of the cars and set their brakes. You could do this by turning a large metal wheel on the platforms on the ends of the cars. That way, if I was in town when the train came to pick up the cars, the train workers would yell and fuss because the brakes were set and they had to turn the wheel to release them.

That was about all I could think of to do there, so I thought I had better go see if Charles was home. I did not want to lie to Mother. I knew she would ask me if I saw Charles.

Charles was not doing anything, but he really did not want to go anywhere like the creek. He was a little upset because I had set all the breaks on the railroad cars without him helping.

So, I headed my bike back toward the house. I was getting a little hungry, and I knew there was some food left from dinner. Sunday dinner leftovers were always good.

A Goose Dinner

One day my older sister, Juanita, and I were walking to town, probably to Sheffield's store. After we had walked across the creek bridge, I wanted to walk up on the mill yard to the old mill pond just to see if there were any ducks. Sometimes during the winter months, ducks would stop in the pond. Juanita was not excited about walking up a little hill just to look at a pond. I begged and she relented. When I was with her away from home, I had to sort of mind her or get in trouble when she told Mother I would not listen to her.

The pond was up a slight hill. We walked slowly up the hill to the pond being quiet so if any ducks were in the pond, we would not scare them away. As we reached where we could see the water in the pond, there was one Ring Neck Canadian goose floating on the water. We quietly went back out of sight so the goose would not fly away. This was an unusual happening. The Canadian geese did not come there very often.

I convinced Juanita to stay and watch the goose, and I would run back to the house and get a shotgun. It took a lot of talking to convince her that my plan was what we should do. (The house was about one-half mile away.)

I remember telling her how good the goose and dressing would be. In my mind, I could smell the aroma of that goose roasting in Mother's oven. The kitchen would smell heavenly to a hungry boy.

I think I must have run most of the way back home. When I got there and told Mother what I wanted, she had lots of questions about me taking the shotgun and carrying it all the way back to the mill yard and shooting the goose. She gave me a thorough lecture about how to carry the shotgun and how to load it and shoot. I knew those things, but she was being a protective mother. I know now that there was probably not much meat at home. I am sure this helped her to agree with my plan to try and get the goose.

She also wanted to know about what she had sent us to the store to get. How did we plan to do that. I told her I would stay out of the store and look after the shotgun and goose. I was sure we were going to get the goose.

I headed back to the mill yard as fast as I could carry the gun and walk. Even though the shotgun was a twenty gauge, it still became heavy for me before I got back to where Juanita was.

When I got back, Juanita was sitting on the ground near the pond. We had a discussion about who was going to shoot the goose. We knew that we would get only one chance at it. I reminded her how many times I had been hunting and brought back squirrels to eat. Afte discussing it for a little, we finally came to an agreement as to who was going to be the shooter. I do not remember who shot the goose, but I knew the pond was very shallow and I could wade out to get the goose. So, I began to wade out to where the goose was floating to get it. Juanita was continually yelling at me to hurry before someone came by and saw what we had.

I retrieved the goose, and we continued toward the store to get what we had been sent to get.

Knowing that we could not take the goose with us into town because we did not know if it was legal to kill a goose at that time of the year, we decided to hide the goose in some thick bushes near the road as we headed on toward the store. We went on to the store. I stayed outside the store with the shotgun while Juanita went inside to get whatever it was that mother had sent us to the store for.

With the groceries, we started back toward the house. When we reached the place where we had hidden the goose, we looked all around to be sure no one was walking the road that could see what we had. I grabbed the goose, and we hightailed it across the creek bridge and turned on the lower road toward the house. We were in a wooded area almost immediately. No one had seen what we had done.

I believe that was the longest half mile I ever walked. The shotgun and goose together were very heavy to me. Juanita was carrying the groceries. I continued to think I was hearing something coming through the woods toward us. The Game Warden had previously sent word to my brother and me that he was going to arrest us if we did not stop squirrel hunting out of season. I did not want him to see what we had. But I knew that he rode a big white horse while in the woods and made lots of noise. Juanita kept telling me to stop worrying, she was tired of hearing it.

When we got home, mother was glad we made it back safely. I could tell she had been worried about two of her children off alone with a gun. I understand more about things like that now than I did then. I do not remember being concerned about what she might be feeling while we were trying to get a goose. That, I think, is part of being young. As I have gotten older and have children of my own, I understand more of those types of feelings and worry.

Mother immediately began dressing the goose. That evening, we had the most awesome meal of goose and dressing.

Willis Payne

There was a gentleman who lived in Roganville while I was growing up. He lived in town on the street from the church toward the post office. As far as I know, he was a confirmed bachelor. He did not like a lot of people around at one time. When it came to holidays like Thanksgiving or Christmas, he went to the river bottom and camped until all the celebrations were over.

He lived in a small frame house with a front porch that had rocking chairs on it. Many times, when I would walk past there going to church or school, there would be some other man sitting on the porch with him. His yard was very neat all around the house. There was not a sprig of grass in the yard anywhere. He lived there into the 1960s, and he still kept the grass out of the yard. He did not believe that grass belonged in a yard.

The last time I remember seeing him was after I was grown. Dad asked me to drive him to Roganville to see

Willis. They sat on the porch of his little house for a couple of hours talking and laughing.

Now, let's continue with the story of Willis.

Willis was a mystery to some of the folks in town. Some thought he was lazy and shiftless. Some thought he was crazy. But I can tell you he was saner than a lot of folks I have known. He wore denim overalls all the time. He was an excellent carpenter. He could do structure or finish carpentry. When he ran low on money, he would work for a few months, or ever how long it took, to replenish his funds.

Willis was a very good cook. That upset some of the busy body ladies in town. I think it may have been because he would not tell anyone how he made any of his dishes. He was extremely generous when someone needed a meal because of illness or whatever problems. He would very often cook and take something to those who needed it.

One of his famous things to cook was cake. A very simple cake with lots of fruit in it. Even though it had lots of fruit, it was still light and extremely tasty. It did not have a name; it was just Willis Payne's cake.

Some of the ladies wanted his recipe. He would just smile and tell them it was just a cake. I have heard ladies talking in groups about how shiftless Willis was, but the conversation always came around to his cake recipe. They would ask if anyone knew how he kept it so light with all the fruit in it. I do not believe anyone ever got the recipe.

In the Neches River bottom, Willis found a place on the Neches River that was great for a camp. It was west of Magnolia Springs and north of highway 190 by a few miles. There was a high spot on the riverbank that would not flood even in extremely high water. At this place, a creek converged with the river. It was called Spring Creek. So, the location was called "the mouth of Spring Creek." This was before Dam B was constructed. After Dam B was constructed, this area was underwater.

Willis constructed a camp house out of scrap lumber and tin he had found somewhere. He had an old coal oil stove that he cooked on if he could not cook outside because of the weather. He had an old wood burning heater that would keep the camp house warm enough to stay in. He was usually there during late fall and early winter.

Men from town would bring him building materials or anything else he needed. As far as I know, he never made any agreements with anyone. He just made him a camp on the river. He and my dad knew about this place.

I heard Dad and Mother talking about a place in the river bottom that they referred to as "the mouth of Spring Creek." I think this was in a conversation of Dad telling Mother about Willis having found him a place on the river to build a camp. Dad was familiar with where this spot on the river was located. I think he helped Willis select that spot.

There were no designated roads into this area. I do not remember exactly how we went to get there. I know we went west from Magnolia Springs on some dirt roads and finally just picked our way through the woods, staying on high ground away from mudholes. Sometimes we had to stop and remove a small tree or an old log that had fallen since the last person drove through there. Dad knew exactly how to get to the camp. Then others would follow the same tracks in. Soon there was a makeshift road to the camp from county roads. This camp was there for a number of years.

Almost every weekend someone from town would go to Willis' camp, so there were always people bringing things, like ice, that he needed.

In warm weather, men would take their teenagers to Willis' camp on some of the weekends. They would gather all the teens that wanted to go to the woods and camp out. The youngsters loved to go. Some of the mothers were not so sure. They still did not like Willis very much.

The teens would have a great time Saturday and spend the night in the woods with all the night animals making their noises. And, of course, Willis would tell tall tales to them late in the evening.

For a meal on Saturday, Willis and the men would make a mulligan stew with whatever the men had brought with them. If someone had killed a couple of squirrels that morning, they went into the mulligan. Sometime the men would have good luck fishing and Willis would fry a bunch of fish.

There were a number of small lakes and an old river channel plus the river itself to fish in. Fish were abundant in most of the waters.

The teenagers had such a fun and happy time. At night they would sit around and sing songs and Willis would tell stories. Some of the older boys and men would set a few trout lines in the river to catch catfish.

It was morning, I was in a boat with Dad and Willis. We stopped where a trout line was tied to a limb of a tree. The limb was moving up and down. One of the men grabbed the line and started to pull it in. Something big was on the line. I remember looking over the side of the boat as the fish came to the surface. I thought the fish was as long as the boat. It was not quite that long, but long enough. We towed the fish back to the riverbank at the camp so someone could get it out of the water. I sure did not want that fish in the boat with me. It was a river blue catfish. It sure did make some good fish steaks when the men fried some of it that day for lunch.

There were other trips I made to Willis' camp. The most enjoyable times I remember were trips in the fall. It was cool at night and early morning. The afternoons were warm and pleasant.

In the early mornings, after a breakfast of fried squirrel or rabbit and fried eggs, someone would start a big pot of stew. The stew pot hung on a rack over a campfire. They would start a fire and get it where it would burn slow and not get the pot too hot.

We then started off squirrel hunting. I still remember the sounds of all the different birds singing and chirping as we walked quietly through the woods. We would separate into small groups and hunt for a few hours. It was easy to know if anyone had seen squirrels by the sound of gunshots. I was not old enough that I could carry a gun. I was good for walking around to the other side of a tree to make the squirrel go back to the side the hunter was on. It was called "turning" the squirrel.

When we made it back to camp, the stew was just about ready. Some of the men would start skinning the squirrels. As soon as the hide was off, someone would call me and hand me a pan with the squirrels in it. My job was to go down to the edge of the river or creek and wash the meat to get all the hair or any foreign stuff off them.

While we were cleaning the squirrels, Willis was making a big pan of cornbread to eat with the stew. Soon the cornbread was done, and we all sat down on a log or stump and ate too much.

After a short rest/nap it was time to go white perch fishing. There was an old river channel nearby. Willis had a boat in it. We had some bait from a minnow trap in the creek. We fished from the bank or some in the boat. We caught a big string of white perch.

I think I slept most of the way back to Roganville.

Wash/Laundry Day

When I was a boy, we had no electricity or running water. Wash day was a big deal. I remember it being on Monday if the weather was dry since the clothes had to be hung on a clothesline.

If I was to go to school that day, I was expected to gather enough firewood and place it near the big cast iron pot where the water was heated for the laundry. Along with the wood, there had to be some kindling to get the fire started. The best kindling was pieces of rich lightered pine. We used a hatchet to chop the rich pine into splinters. The splinters would burn easily with a match. So, a little pile of the splinters with firewood on top of them would start a fire under the washpot.

Kindling

Rich lightered pine was parts of a pine tree that had been cut and left in the woods or a pine tree that fallen or knocked down by weather. As the wood of a green pine tree lay in the woods, there were insects and worms that would eat away the outside layers of the wood and leave the heart of the piece intact. The heart of a pine tree contains a lot of turpentine.

The insects will not eat that part. As the left-over part of the pine tree ages, it becomes very dry and the turpentine concentrates in the wood that is left. This process takes a number of years. Pieces of this rich pine will burn as if it was soaked in a solvent.

Left in the outdoors, it will not rot. Gathering this rich pine became a popular way of making a living for some people in the 1950s and 60s. The rich pine was gathered and sold to a company that recovered the turpentine from it. The tree stumps left from logging of the pine trees years before, were solid rich lightered pine. Gatherers would use power equipment to pull the stumps out.

As I wandered through the woods, I would pick up pieces and carry them home. They were always needed to start fires in the fireplace or in the kitchen wood stove.

Wash / Laundry Day

After we had a fire going under the washpot, I had to hurry to draw some water from the well to put in the wash pot before it became too hot. This took a little while because there had to be enough hot water for Mother to put some in a wash tub to scrub white clothes and enough to refill a wash tub when the water cooled off. After the sheets and white clothes, then the darker fabrics were washed. The wash and rinse tubs sat on a "wash bench" near the wash pot. We would move the bench depending on wind direction.

When the wind blew the smoke from the fire under the washpot toward the wash bench, it had to be moved to keep the smoke out of Mother's eyes while she washed and also to keep the clothes from smelling like smoke.

I also drew enough water to fill another wash tub to be used as rinse water. After the clothes were scrubbed on a rub board, they were rinsed in clear water, then squeezed out and hung on a clothesline.

It does not take long to say what took a half day to accomplish. The fresh sheets and other clothing smelled so very fresh and clean after drying in the sunshine.

I did not realize how hard mother worked until I was a lot older. After hanging all the laundry, she then would start an evening meal. The evening meal (supper) usually included biscuits and sometimes cornbread served with the meal, all of it cooked on a wood burning stove.

After a few years, I remember Dad brought home a coal oil (kerosene) cook stove. It made it so much easier for mother not to have to build fires in the wood stove. Dad would complain that the food tasted like coal oil. It really did not, but the fumes from the burning coal oil did cause a rancid odor in the kitchen if it was cold and Mother could not open the kitchen to breezes.

First Washing Machine

After my older sister, Juanita, finished school, she went to work in Kirbyville for the electric co-op. She was a secretary in their office.

She purchased a washing machine driven by a gasoline engine for Mother. It was put on the back porch just outside the kitchen door. I did not think Mother would be able to start the engine on the machine, but she surprised me as she did many times.

The washer would agitate the clothes and then with the engine still running the clothes could be run through a wringer into a tub of rinse water. Then run back through the ringer to a clean tub or basket, from there they would then be hung on the clothesline.

Hot water still had to be carried around the house to the back porch where the washing machine was placed. Mother did not want it outside where rain and trash could blow into it. It was still hard work, but with the washing machine, she did not have to use a rub board. This made it a little easier for her. I can remember trying to get her to wait until Saturday so I could be there all day while she was washing.

The washing machine engine made so much noise we had to shout to be heard by someone else if we were on the back porch. The thing vibrated so much it would move about on the porch. It had wheels on it that locked in place, but it was necessary to place pieces of wood or something to keep it from moving toward the edge of the porch. Once, Mother even tied a rope around it and attached the rope to the wall to keep it where it was supposed to be. It was a lot of trouble to use, but it was a lot easier for her. We had a lot of laughs during the time we used that crazy washing machine.

A Memorable Christmas

As I sit here writing this, it is Christmas season of 2023. I remember many Christmases when I was a boy, but there is one that stands out in my memory. I think it was in the mid-1940s, because Dad had struggled to find a steady job. There was almost no construction going on for a few years after World War II. So times were hard. I heard discussions between Mom and Dad about how to make enough money to pay our grocery bill at Sheffield's store.

Now about Christmas at our house. Usually there were a few gifts for each of the children. I usually received a metal car and a cap pistol with holster. There was always fruit and some Christmas candy on the dining table when we awakened Christmas morning.

This Christmas there was no fruit or candy. There were no presents for anyone. Mom told us that there just was not any money to spend on gifts this year. It did not bother me at all. I still had plenty of snuff bottle cars, my sling shot and pocketknife to keep me busy. I think our parents were hurt worse by it than the kids were.

Mother announced that we were going to Papa Wright's for Christmas. I knew there would be plenty of food and Papa would be telling his stories. He loved to tell stories about when he was young. I certainly enjoyed hearing them. I knew I would get to see Papa use his whip and show me the deer hides he was tanning and maybe a new whip he was plaiting. He always had some new project going on using tanned deer leather.

Also, since we were going to Papa Wright's, we would get to cross the river on the ferry located between Magnolia Springs and Spurger. That was always fun for me to ride the ferry. Not for Mother. She did not like to ride the ferry.

We crossed the ferry. We were singing Christmas songs and just having a great time. Everyone had completely forgotten there were no gifts that morning. Even my dad was singing along with us. He had a good bass voice.

As we got closer to Papa's house, I really got excited. Then as we drove up to the house, there were no cars or people in sight. There was no smoke coming from the fireplace chimney. It was obvious no one was home. We drove just down the road where Mom and Dad could see Aunt Annie's house. She was my dad's oldest sister. The front yard was full of cars of all his siblings. Dad recognized some of the cars and knew who they belonged to.

Things went downhill from there. Mother and Dad had not been notified that his family would get together at Aunt Annie's and Uncle Claude's house. Dad was very angry, probably hurt more than angry. His siblings sort of pushed him aside when they could. Mother told him that it was OK with her if he wanted us to stop and join his family. His answer was HELL NO.

As soon as Dad could find a place to turn the car around, he did. No one was talking as we started back the way we had just come. When we got back to Papa's house, instead of just passing by, Dad stopped and started to get out of the car and Mother asked him what he was going to do. He said he was going to leave them a note, so they knew we had come. He mumbled something about never coming here again. But we did go back at a later time.

Dad got back in the car, and we started back toward Spurger. I thought, "I get to ride the ferry again." Riding the ferry was fun. When the ferry was first pulled off the bank, it began to drift down river with the current. It made me think it was going to float down the river. As soon as the slack in the cable was gone, it stopped drifting down river and began to move toward the other bank. (I know I have written in another story about how the ferry was moved, but if you're randomly reading the book, it bears repeating.) The ferry was moved by manpower from a man with a long club that he hooked on the cable and walked toward the opposite end of the ferry. The ferry moved along using rollers on the cable that stretched across the river. The cable was anchored to trees on the riverbanks. If the river water level was high, it took quite an effort to pull the ferry along to the other bank.

I was enjoying the ride across the river. You could hear the water sloshing against the ferry boat as it floated. Sometimes you could see a fish jump in the river. It was exciting for me. But everyone in the car was quiet. No singing or even conversation. I do not know what others were thinking, but I was wondering where and what we were going to eat. I knew Mother had made some chicken and dressing from a hen she dressed the day before to bring with us. That was always good, so I did not worry much about eating anymore. I just enjoyed the ferry ride.

Earlier when we had first reached the ferry, I heard the ferry man ask Dad, "Why are you back so soon?" I do not know what their conversation was, but it was not very long. As soon as we docked on the other side, Dad got in the car and we started up the other riverbank in quite a hurry.

I wondered which way Dad would take to go back home. Probably through Magnolia Springs. My Aunt Mae and Uncle Webster lived there. Their son, Kenneth, was one of my best buddies. I knew if we stopped there, Kenneth and I would do something fun like try to kill rats in the corn crib with a broom handle or walk into the woods near their house. We always found fun things to do together.

The road we would take in Magnolia Springs went right by Aunt Mae's house. Sure enough, Mother asked Dad if we could stop so they could wish her sister and brother-in-law Merry Christmas. Dad said OK, but we are not going to stay long.

We stopped and everybody hugged everybody else. Kenneth and I immediately headed out toward the barn. Dad yelled at me to stay put because we were going on home in a few minutes. Aunt Mae took over the conservation and said "John, just be quiet. Y'all are staying and having Christmas dinner with us. Margie says she has a big pan of chicken and dressing, and she makes the very best. So just hush and you and Webster go sit down in the living room. You boys go play and do not get filthy dirty. We will call you when dinner is ready."

About midday, they called us to come in to dinner. Both families sat around the great big dinner table. Even the children. Aunt Mae did not believe that the children should have to wait for the adults to finish. Mother and Aunt Mae fixed the younger ones their plates. But amazingly enough, we could ask for more if we were still hungry. But if we asked for seconds, we had better eat it or we would be in big trouble.

After dinner was finished and the kitchen was clean, everyone laid and sat around, trying to stay awake. Kenneth and I were too full to go play outside. After a little while, the room started to get quiet. Aunt Mae said, "Let's play and sing." They had a piano. Mother played the piano, Aunt Mae played the Hawaiian Guitar, Uncle Webster played a standard guitar, and Dad sang bass. And did they make some pretty music. All the adults and the teenagers sang as the adults played. Mostly Gospel songs and some Christmas songs. I can remember how beautiful I thought the music sounded.

I was not a believer at that age, but I now know that us being at Aunt Mae and Uncle Webster's house on that Christmas day was directed by our Heavenly Father. My parents had been hurt by being left out, but God intervened in a way that made it a memorable Christmas for them and us kids.

I will always remember the happy singing and carrying on that went on in the car on the way home. No one even noticed there had not been presents. The day had been spent visiting, eating, singing, and enjoying family.

I hope you understand why that Christmas with no presents is so memorable for me.

Our Family's Experience of WW II

I do not have many memories of how WW II impacted our family. I was too young to remember Pearl Harbor being attacked. As I became older, I remember Mother and Dad talking about how the Japs had bombed Pearl Harbor and killed many of our soldiers. They also talked about how bad the Japs treated our soldiers who became prisoners of war.

I had a second cousin who was on the Bataan Death March. His name was Estell Morgan. He was the son of Great Uncle Bruce Morgan. After he came home, he could not go squirrel hunting if anyone carried a shotgun. The noise of the shotgun caused him to turn and run back home. He and my older brother hunted together a great deal. After a while of being back home, they would try to go squirrel hunting, but John Maston had to yell at Estell before shooting even a 22. It took a while before Estell could tolerate even the sound of a 22 rifle.

I remember seeing truckloads of German prisoners being hauled somewhere north of us toward Holly Springs. The trucks came through Roganville going north. I never knew where the camp was. I remember the prisoners did not look afraid. Their clothing was not ragged and torn. It appeared they were treated well.

I also remember the US troops camping not too from our house in the woods. The troops were there on maneuvers. They would spend three days to a week marching and doing whatever maneuvers required. I remember hearing lots of yelling and then total quiet. I often wondered what they were doing. I was told to keep myself at home during these periods. But I really wanted to go see what was going on in the woods, however, I knew the fur would fly if I left the house to go near where the soldiers were.

When the wind was right, I could smell the smoke of their cooking fires. Sometimes I thought I could smell bacon frying. We could not purchase bacon or much sugar. All these items were rationed to the public. Most were kept to feed our soldiers. As a kid, I wondered where they could get that much food to feed a large group of soldiers. I was very young and had never seen an abundance of food.

Any time there was a camp of soldiers on maneuvers, some of the ladies that lived near would cook big pots of chicken and dumplings or pots of stew. The men would take this food to the soldiers. My Dad and others seemed to always know where the soldiers were camped.

When on maneuvers, the soldiers could not give any food, equipment, or tools to the residents. Whatever food that was leftover when they started to leave had to be destroyed or buried.

Most often when the maneuvers were over, people who lived nearby would find a slab of bacon and maybe a sack of sugar or sometimes a sack of white flour on one of the porches of their house. This food was always wrapped and secured so dogs or other animals could not get to it. No one heard anything during the night. The stuff just appeared. Neighbors who were privileged in this way shared this food with neighbors.

Communications were not very good for people living in the rural areas that did not have electricity or a radio. Mother had a nephew serving in the Pacific Theater. His name was Julian Morgan. He did not make it back. His life was taken by a sniper on one of the islands. Mother had also lost an uncle in WW I. His name was Lester Morgan. He was killed on October 13, 1918, just about a month before that war ended.

Dad worked mostly in the shipyards at Orange, Texas or Galveston, Texas. When he worked in Galveston, he was gone from home a week at a time. In today's world, it is hard to think that your spouse is gone for a week at a time and there is no way to communicate. Mother knew the name and phone number of the boarding house where he stayed in Galveston. She could have gotten a message to him if she walked to the post office and asked to use their telephone. Otherwise, she waited each Friday evening for him to come home. They always spent some time together talking after he had come in on Friday afternoon. In that time, a child did not listen to his parents' conversations, but I managed to hear enough to know they were talking about the war.

On the weeks Dad had been working, we would go to the movies in Kirbyville on Saturday. I always hoped for a sunshiny Saturday. Someone would draw a washtub full of water for baths. If the sun was shining, the tub of water would be set in the sunshine to get warm. If not, sometimes it was rather cold. I knew to take a good bath because Mother was going to check my ears to be sure they were clean. It was not pleasant when she had to go back and redo where I had missed some dirt. She did not use the word dirty. She said she would not go anywhere with a boy that had filth in his ears.

I really enjoyed the Batman and Robin serials. There was always a "cliff hanger" with Batman and Robin. I knew what sort of danger they had been in when the movie finished the week before. I thought it was a big problem if we skipped a Saturday at the movies.

The adults went to the movies mainly because they showed some news reels of actual battles that had taken place in this war, and updates of the number of casualties the previous week. I remember the films of fighter planes and bombers dropping bombs on targets. They seldom would say where the films were shot. Sometimes you could see palm trees in some of the films. That usually indicated that film was shot in the South Sea islands.

I did not realize just how horrible the war was. Youth is very forgiving. We were taken care of and had food to eat when we wanted it. It did not seem as traumatic to the children as it really was.

After going to the movies, the next few days I would lie out in some grassy area waiting to see if I could see a war plane flying over. I did not have a "spotter" book, but someone in town had shown me one. I tried to remember what different planes looked like. I remember seeing a few B17 bombers flying over our area.

I was at school the day the war was declared over. The school was turned out for the day.

Trains, Tracks and Hobos

I have talked about my friend Charles Brasher in some of the earlier stories. There were very few boys our age in the community around Roganville, so we spent a lot of our free time together. He lived very near the center of Roganville so it was easy for me to walk or ride my bicycle to town or meet him. We liked to meet near the railroad crossing in town, which was always an interesting place for us to look around for treasures.

Treasures for ten- to twelve-year-old boys could be anything we did not have that was interesting, especially if we could carry it in our pockets. Around the railroad yard where the pulpwood cars were left to be loaded, we could usually find a nickel or two so we could go to the store and buy an RC Cola. (R. C. Cola was the largest drink in the store's coke box.) If we were lucky and found more change, we could get a bag of peanuts to put in the soda. That really made it taste good.

If we were lucky, a freight train would come through while we were there. If there were pulpwood cars loaded and ready to be picked up, it was neat to watch the train workers disconnect the cars to make a place for the loaded pulp wood cars. There was a lot of moving back and forth after they separated the cars and placed them where they wanted them to be.

There were just beginning to be some diesel-powered engines pulling the freight trains. They did not make quite as much noise as the steam driven engines. They were neater and shinier than the old steam engines. With the diesel engines, the engineer was easier to see. There was not a lot of steam blowing around and making noise and spewing hot water and steam. We would wave until the engineer saw us. He would wave back and blow the air horn on the engine. That was neat, but we liked the sound of the steam whistle better.

When we tired of looking around the railroad yard, we would walk the tracts toward Jasper and look for things along the tracks. It seems people who rode the train or the people loading the cars threw all sorts of things away. The hobos would also throw things along side of the tracks. We never found anything that was valuable, but we never gave up trying.

As we walked along the tracks, we always looked at the ends of the railroad ties for the date nails. In the end of each tie, a large nail with the year was driven into the tie. We were always looking for nails with our birth year on them. The further away from town we went, the nails seemed to be older. Maybe the railroad ties were replaced more often near the town.

We would sometimes follow the track for a mile or so. Not too far out of town we would find hobo signs. Hobos left signs for other hobos that pointed in the direction of houses that would give them food. Not everyone would allow hobos to come near their house. Sometimes, they were even shot at, or a shotgun was discharged to scare them away from certain houses.

There was one place where a group of rocks were laid in the form of an arrow pointing in the general direction of where we lived. I think it was possibly because my mom and another lady that lived in that general direction would give them food. We did not have food to spare, but Mother said she could find something so a person would not go hungry. Any house that gave a hobo something to eat would have regular visits by others.

Hobo signs were always just a little ways out of town. The hobos would get off the trains as the train slowed approaching the rail yard. This might be a quarter or half mile out of town.

Sometime Charles and I would try and follow some of the hobo signs. We would occasionally find a place where hobos had made a little camp and probably spent a day or so. The freight trains did not come through every day.

When I noticed it was getting time for me to go home, I would leave the tracks and walk home through the woods. I could cross Thickety Creek on a foot log I knew about. The way the track ran, it was only about three quarters of a mile home. Charles would follow the tracks back to town.

A Scary Trip To Town

As a 13-year-old boy, I had an experience of being in almost total darkness while going to town to get medical help for my mom. I will try to set the context of what was happening at our house around this time.

It was early summer. As I have noted before, our house was really in the woods. It was about a mile to the nearest house. Just a few days before the incident that scared me so badly, we were all sitting on the back porch around dusk. Our parents were sitting in rocking chairs while Robbie and I sat on the porch steps or in a straight chair. We heard the scariest scream we could imagine. It sounded just like a woman screaming at the top of her lungs. Our parents said, "Well, the panther is coming back through."

It seems that about twice a year we would hear this. And it was pretty close to the house. The thought was that the panther traveled from one river bottom to another about twice a year. We were located between Sabine and Neches rivers.

Now, here is the story of how I was so very scared.

I was 13 years old. I had an experience of being in almost total darkness while walking to town to call the doctor to come help my mom. About the only phone in town was at the post office, which was in postmaster's house. My Dad awakened me sometime during the night and told me I had to go to town and get the people who had the phone to call the doctor to come quickly. Then wait to show the doctor how to get to the house.

My mom was very sick and having trouble breathing. My dad was sitting with her in his lap with mom in a position to help her breathe better. This scared me before I really got scared.

It was a dark night. Absolutely no moonlight. As long as I was walking where there were no trees, I could see enough to know where to walk to stay on the trail. Now remember, I kept thinking of the panther we heard scream a couple of nights before. I kept thinking I could hear something walking along beside the trail I was following. I would stop frequently, and I thought I would hear one step in the leaves after I stopped. I couldn't see well enough to run, so I walked fast.

One part of the walk to town went through a section that was very dense with beech trees. That night was a dark night with absolutely no moon at all. The only way I could tell where I was walking was to look at the tree trunks. Their bark was almost white, so they were visible. I knew from memory where the trail was through the trees. I didn't know if I was walking near snakes or what.

I was frightened. I was sure I heard something following me. But I knew I had to keep going. After about a quarter of a mile, I came out of the dense trees, and I could see where I was walking from the starlight. It was an extreme relief. I think I ran the rest of the way to town.

Everything worked out OK. The doctor came and I rode back home with him to show him the way. He gave Mom some medicine and she began to get better. I never should have let myself get so frightened. I knew I wasn't in danger. But I could not see what was around me.

I was afraid of something I couldn't see. This is something we should never do.

My First Job

Soon after the episode when my mom was so sick, we moved to town from my grandfather's house. The doctor told my dad that if he wanted my mom to live, he would have to get her out of the woods to an easier life with a few conveniences. So, we moved to town.

This was in the summertime. I was so shy I could hardly talk to anyone. I made one friend that lived next to the apartment that Dad had rented, with Juanita's help. During the next month, my new friend and I would ride our bikes back to Roganville at least once each week.

The rest of the summer is vague to my memories.

I wanted to get a job. I was fourteen. I talked to Dad about it. He told me that I did not have to work, but if I did I could have more things I wanted that he may not be able to afford.

Being so shy, I did not know how I was going to ask someone for a job. It was getting to the time school had started. I heard that the grocery store in town wanted help for cleaning up each evening. I managed to get enough courage to go ask about the job. The first thing I found out was that age 14 was not old enough to have a job unless my parents completed and signed a "Minor's Release" for me to work. All the paperwork got done (don't remember how) and I got a job.

Then I found out the job was working in the meat market. I soon found out that things in a meat market got rather dirty and messy. Everything had to be cleaned spotlessly every evening before the store closed. So, after school I went to work at the store each day til 6 PM Monday thru Friday and all day on Saturday.

I was now a "Town Boy." The barefoot boy no longer existed.

CLOSING REMARKS

My efforts that drove this project was to impart some information and descriptions of how I lived as a boy to my grand and great grandchildren just for knowledge and fun.

As I close this project, I would be remis if I did not include what I think my definition of love is. I am sure it's probably different than when I was 12 or 13 years old. I believe that true love only comes from Almighty God. He gave His only Son as a sacrifice for our sins so that there might be a way by which we can have life everlasting. Eternal life cannot be bought or earned. It is truly a gift from our Creator.

God's desire is to have a loving relationship with each of us. This growth of this love relationship is up to us. We must really believe in our hearts that God does, in fact, love us so much that His Son Jesus died on a cross, was buried, and rose on the third day. He suffered and died for our sins. God loves us so much that when we believe and accept Jesus as our Savior, God then adopts us into His family, and we can never be separated from Him. Jesus said that we are in Him and He is in the Father, so that makes it impossible for us to ever be separated from God.

Love is an incredibly living vibrant thing, and within love itself there are a whole bunch of different kinds of love.

There's non-romantic platonic love between friends, love between family members, plus intense unconditional love. But, most often, when people talk about love, they mean romantic love with a spouse.

True love with a spouse is the next step down from the love we experience with God. God ordained marriage. Then when children are born, love for them is almost indescribable. Yet, Abraham was going to sacrifice his son because God asked him to. But God's love provided a sacrificial lamb.

When my son was about 3 years old, he asked his mom, "Do you love Jesus more than me." I do not know what her answer was, but I do know that when we love God unconditionally, the Holy Spirit will provide an answer.

We truly experience love more when we have experienced the love of God in our lives. Since all love originates with God, it stands to reason that our love with others will be more intense after experiencing God's love.

Love is not a noun. Love is a verb or action word. If we truly care for others, we will express it by doing for them, whether it be children, grandchildren, other family, or friends.

In our world today, the word "love" is misused so very much. Many people use love to describe everything from food to activities. I try not to do that. I like food, I do not love it. Love is reserved for God, family, church family, friends, and neighbors. If you think about it, that is all people. It is much easier to understand this as we age, I think.

May God bless and keep each person who looks at this book. I truly hope I have said nothing to hurt or upset any person.

May God bless and keep each of you.

ABOUT THE AUTHOR

Dale R. Wright, Sr.

At 87 years of age, Dale Wright has penned his first book. His goal is to preserve some of his boyhood memories in story form for his grand and great grandchildren. His hope is for them to see the contrast of how he lived as a youngster versus how they live today and to gain enjoyment from reading the stories.

www.ingramcontent.com/pod-product-compliance
Lightning Source LLC
Chambersburg PA
CBHW061155120626
46546CB00005B/2077